TWO NATURES IN CONFLICT

Winning Over Fleshly Battles

The more serious you are about living for the Lord, the more temptations Satan tends to hurl at you. Never be frustrated or faint in your mind.

BISHOP EPHRAIM J. UDOFIA

PENDIUM
PUBLISHING HOUSE
514-201 DANIELS STREET
RALEIGH, NC 27605

For information, please visit our Web site at
www.pendiumpublishing.com

PENDIUM Publishing and its logo
are registered trademarks.

Two Natures In Conflict
By Dr. Ephraim J. Udofia

ISBN: 978-1-936513-55-0

Cover design by GloryCreative Group, Inc.
(glorycreativegroup@gmail.com)

PUBLISHER'S NOTE

**Unless otherwise stated, all scripture references are taken from the
King James Version of the Bible.**

This book is printed on acid-free paper.

Dedication

What a Christian Brother and friend, Elder Cleveland Hughes, your love, financial support to the work in my hand is worthy of all commendation. Thanks for being there in all seasons of our life's experiences, as we fight to win over the fleshly battles together these thirty and some years, still counting.

Praise for Two Natures In Conflict

Wow, *Two Natures in Conflict, Winning over Fleshly Battles* helps us understand our total self and view ourselves as God really sees us. "Where there is life, there are possibilities. None of us was created for failure, but for a divine purpose." The book reveals the devil's schemes so we know what to be aware of. And, not only that, it shows us how to walk and live victoriously in this present world in order to make Heaven. This book is a must read. Allow it to change your life and give you victory over the old nature. I encourage every believer to purchase this book.

Your friend and brother,
Pastor Ronald Wayne Sharpe
Powerhouse Church of Jesus Christ, Inc.
Raleigh, North Carolina

Dr. Udofia spiritual insight on critical issues confronting our human nature in our relationship with God is completely filled with the revelation given to him by the Holy Spirit. In this book, the author unveils the two natures are in constant conflicts with each other. It is not a guess work, but real biblical truth. It's hard to argue with biblical truth and the voice of experience. By reading this book, your spirit will be enhanced to uncover the hidden truths that will propel you to the next level of glory. I highly recommend *Two Natures in Conflict* to every born-again Christian who wants to experience daily victory in Christ Jesus.

Anietie Affiah, Senior Pastor
Faith In Christ Church Worldwide
Durham, North Carolina

I believe the book entitled, *Two Natures in Conflict* will be a blessing to your spiritual walk with Christ. It will help you to understand the battles that you are confronted with daily in your Christian journey with Christ. The author, Dr. Ephraim J. Udofia has been anointed by God to help God's children to defeat the devil and be more than a conqueror through Jesus Christ. It will be a blessing to your spiritual man and help you to understand the natural man by allowing us to grow in Christ Jesus. May God bless you and keep you in his Divine will.

A Servant of the Master
Suffragan Bishop Phillip J. Knox
Gospel Mission Apostolic Church
Charleston, South Carolina

Contents

Foreword

B ishop Udofia is my friend and colleague in ministry. Since meeting him several years ago, I have not met a finer man in heart and spirit, in character, personality or integrity. He is a humble man, in spite of the loftiness of his dignity and wisdom. I have deep and abiding veneration for the work he does for the Body of Christ. God has anointed him with kindness, grace and compassion for lost souls, which has carried him around the world ministering to people, even while endangering his own life. He uses his own money and the support of others to finance his evangelistic campaigns. He shares the gospel of JESUS CHRIST with a fresh and innovative approach. He "thinks outside the box," which allows his philosophy to be unhindered by traditional dogma and legalistic concepts widely accepted by many who pursue holiness by keeping a set of rules.

Most of the time we read books written by people we may never meet in person, but I have read practically every book Bishop Udofia has written. All of them, spiritual masterpieces eloquently written with a spirit of excellence, which in my opinion, is the key to success! However, this literary work, TWO NATURES IN CONFLICT, is the best work he has ever published. Its approach to the psychology of the dichotomy of man gives the reader an opportunity not only to know the Aurthor, but to know and understand himself. Enormous insight into the human condition is given to Bishop Udofia. He explores both the natural and spiritual entities of the human conscience and spiritual being of man. In this book, spiritual truths confront human realities and reveal biblical concepts that give victory to the Believer. Instruction in righteousness is the intent of the Author and these truths are immensely important to the Believer's walk with God [A word of caution to the readers of this book for—the instruction you obey becomes the future you create . . .]

Furthermore, the simplicity of his message reveals the power of his passion to give hope to every Believer who struggles with himself, within himself, to be without himself and yet needing himself to be himself. There are people you can't live with them and you can't live without them. Thus, we must contend with the TWO NATURES. Bishop Udofia has given us a biblical perspective of a paradoxical, but not impossible situation that exists in the life of every Believer but can be overcome. The practical application of God's word will give any man power to win over fleshly battles.

The Believer, who approaches Bishop Udofia's book with expectancy in his heart, will ultimately find victory in knowing that *"He that spared not His own Son, but delivered Him up for us all, how shall He not with Him also freely give us all things?" (Romans 8:32). Reading this book made me realize that GOD must have loved me more than He loved His own Son. Otherwise, He would have spared His own Son and allowed me to die. Instead, He "delivered Him up for us all, how shall He not with Him also freely give us all things." God* gave us an advantage over every opposing spirit and over all the power (authority) of the enemy (Luke 10:19).

Bishop Udofia is not a novice, but an experienced, well-matured, well-seasoned and well-done man of God. He conveys a message in this book that should compel every Believer to go back to the basic rudiments of his faith and pray for the anointing that empowers us to become ambassadors for Christ. Be well assured, the grip of the flesh, the carnal mind and the lust thereof is no laughing matter (James 1:14, 15). Nevertheless, the remedy that Bishop Udofia offers is simple but powerful—"*you must be born again*" (John 3:3-7). Paul said: "There is therefore now no condemnation to them which are in Christ Jesus, who walk not after the flesh, but after the Spirit. For the law of the Spirit of life in Christ Jesus hath made me free from the law of sin and death" (Romans 8:1-2). "Therefore if any man be in Christ, he is a new creature: old things are passed away; behold, all things are become new" (II Corinthians 5:17). You must read this book to learn from the Word of God, the spiritual strategies designed for victorious living!

Bishop Marion E. Wright, Sr., Ph.D.

Senior Pastor of Greater Emmanuel Temple of Grace

Durham, North Carolina

Gratitude

Time and space will not permit me to list all those whose love, prayer, kind words, and support directly and indirectly have been the cushion to rest my head upon. That notwithstanding, I wish to express my heartfelt appreciation to the following:

My deceased parents: my father, Captain John Udofia of Salvation Army and my compassionate mother, Nko John Udofia. They raised me right with strict discipline and moral values. Both were entrepreneurs in their own rights, who ran successful businesses and had a house full of servants.

My wife, prayer partner, and friend "Precious". For over 34 years we have pressed onward by faith sustained in the riches of his grace. Thanks for being the mother of many.

My esteemed editor, my daughter, intercessor and faithful laborer, Princess Glory E. Udofia.

My able secretary of more than 24 years, the fingers behind these pages. Your patience has been remarkable all these years. Thanks!

Bishop Marion E. Wright, Sr., of Greater Emmanuel Temple of Grace, Durham, North Carolina.

Bishop Maxie Dobson and his church family at Temple of Miracles, Fayetteville, North Carolina.

Living Faith Apostolic Ministries' Pastors, Evangelists, Elders, Deacons, Ministers, leaders and church family home and abroad.

Senior Pastor Anietie Affiah and the saints of Faith in Christ Church Worldwide, Durham, North Carolina.

Pastor Ronald W. Sharpe and church family of Powerhouse Church of Jesus Christ, Raleigh, North Carolina.

INTRODUCTION

I t's obvious that if you're reading this as a 'REAL' Christian, who has surrendered your life to the Lordship of Jesus Christ, you've had your share of conflicts between the old and the new nature. Before Jesus came into our lives, we all lived our lives to pacify the pangs of our old nature. As the scripture says, we were sold under sin and could do no better. "There's none that does good, no, not one." From hands-on experience, you know these conflicts are ongoing, and are not over. Therefore, there's no room to be laggard in our walk and life of faith.

Two Natures in Conflict is written to arm you with the right response principles in living a victorious Christian life, notwithstanding the ongoing battles. This book will be your compass to navigate the torrential terrains in this war within our natures. Our journey together through this literary work is to (a) unmask those subtle areas in our lives that give us grave concerns, (b) identify biblical precepts that are relevant, and (c) confront them with faith and verity and emerge a victorious Christian.

One of the great obstacles is the undeniable desire of the old nature. We were born with it and cannot, by our power, overcome this trait. King David said in Psalm 51:5, "Behold, I was shapen in iniquity; and in sin did my mother conceive me." This was an acknowledgment by King David rather than an excuse. As a man after God's own heart, who sought to please God with his whole heart, his transgression with Bathsheba was a shocking reality of the old nature.

Apostle Paul puts it this way, "For the good that I would I do not: but the evil which I would not, that I do. Now if I do that I would not, it is no more I that do it, but sin that dwelleth in me. (Romans 7:19-20). Both statements reveal the truth of this vicious conflict that wars in our nature.

The deep felt remorse from King David informs us of how genuine this man's standing was with God. Out of this bitter experience, King David penned one of the most powerful Psalms of repentance in the Bible—Psalm 51. I beseech you to read it as time permits. It is a great uplifting Psalm of penitence.

King David's Heartfelt Petition to God

- Besought his enduring mercy
- Pleaded for thorough cleansing
- Saw the sin he committed for what is was—didn't rationalize it nor lightly shove it aside.
- Desired a righteous spirit and clean heart

I see in his approach the true action of a child of God who has discovered the folly of the old nature and the power of our new nature created in Christ Jesus our Lord. This gives us comfort in that King David won over this plight and never became a victim to this nature again through the rest of his kingship. There's hope of winning over the old nature through genuine repentance, total surrender, and a desire to be filled with the power of the Holy Spirit.

Yes, we can win over this conflict and live our lives to the glory of the Lord Jesus Christ. We must consider ourselves dead to sin but alive to God by the renewing of the Holy Ghost. Let's beware that Satan is not afraid of our denominational names but only bows to the name of Jesus Christ and the power of his shed blood. Only by the cleansing of Jesus' blood and his indwelling spirit in our lives, can we have dominion over the old, demanding, selfish, and sinful nature that lurks within our being.

Dr. C. I. Scofield reasoned in this regards, "As we received human nature by natural generation, so do we receive the divine nature by regeneration." The Lord does not impose upon our old nature but rather gives us a completely new nature which, "after God is created in righteousness and true holiness."

This is a spiritual birth that transcends human comprehension. Jesus calls it being "born again of the water and of the spirit." It's in this nature that we have a new standing with God, though natural human beings. We enter into a new covenant of life and victory, no longer to live our lives only by the yearnings of our flesh—old nature.

You're taking an exciting journey as you read along. Read with an open heart and prayer, not with preconceived, human bias. This book will reveal precepts of living an overcoming life to you. Read it over, meditate upon those pointers that stand out to you, and apply them in your daily, Christian living with faith and confidence.

My prayer for you is that your life be an aroma of goodness and righteousness as you shine as a light in our dark, lost world.

Dr. Ephraim J. Udofia

Chapter One

Happy Birthday

"That which is born of the flesh is flesh; and
that which is born of the spirit is spirit" (John 3:6).

After the fall of man in the Garden of Eden, the pronouncement of God's judgment on the parties for their transgressions, Adam and Eve departed to fulfill God's command of "Be fruitful, multiply and replenish the earth, and subdue it . . . ," They were to celebrate many happy birthdays of their children. The irony was that these children were now to be born and shared in the sinful nature of their parents. They had no choice, alternative, nor say so in this matter. Likewise, we have none either. All humans, whatever their claims may be, are of one original set of parents and therefore descendants of Adam and Eve. The Bible says "And hath made of one blood all nations of men for to dwell on all the face of the earth, and hath determined the times before appointed, and the bounds of their habitation. (Acts 17:26).

This is our pedigree; hence you and I share in the same nature of good and evil. Yes, it's a Happy Birthday to be born into the

1

world; millions had no chance, but you are here. We are born with a conscience which is the candle of the Lord in all humans to discern right or wrong. It makes no difference what your belief as touching creation may be. We all have a conscience, whether we obey it or not, or activate or deaden it, this is our choice. God said, "My spirit shall not always strive with man, for that he also *is* flesh: yet his days shall be an hundred and twenty years." (Genesis 6:3).

We are not robots. God did not intend for us to be such. We are born into the world with a free will, a power of choice, ability to make decisions, and as I alleged to earlier, with a conscience. This is the divine design, yet it comes with higher responsibility and accountability. God's spirit will not fight us, force us, nor super impose himself upon us. Our serving him must be born out of free will, love and choice. I've heard people say, why doesn't God make us serve him? That's the problem of that old nature of ours. To our thinking, it must be God's fault that we don't serve him. This is human nature. It started from the Garden of Eden with Adam. It's not surprising that the conflict rages on.

As the adventure through life continues, our future birthdays are met with joy, sadness, optimism, regret, etc. depending on the decisions and choices we have begun to make. I often wonder which school a toddler attended, that you can catch them right in the act, but they will lie to you, that it was not them that committed the offence. None of us is exonerated from this, though as adults, we may think we did not act in like manner. Don't you wish that were true? You would've been an angel right out of your mother's womb. I'm sorry to say we all have that Adamic nature to deal with which cannot be wished or prayed away.

Yes, I know that there are many non-happy birthdays wherein a child is born, due to the circumstances that surround that birth. To that child, before God, it's a happy birthday because "Where there is life, there are possibilities." You will not be here to judge otherwise, if your parents did not allow you to see the light of life. So it's a Happy Birthday in spite of whatever. The formative years of growing up impact upon our ability to live a promising life. "Train up a child in the way he should go: and when he is old, he will not depart from it" (Proverbs 22:6).

Now, since we are not the creator, it's proper and wise if we obey, not debate, the divine instruction and leave the rest for God's execution. Divine order outlives human ingenuities. It benefits and is applicable in all human civilizations. God plays no partiality. His grace and mercy endures to all generations. Obviously, you must have discovered a lot of this about yourself by now. I hope this is true, as this will bring you to a proper perspective of what being human entails. Notwithstanding, these conflicting struggles within our nature, none of us was created for failure. God has endowed upon each of us an inalienable right to attain usefulness and productive living if we choose to. The natural birth brings us into the human family, not into the animal kingdom. There may be those who choose to differ from this statement. That's alright. The Lord has allowed them that choice. Whatever the case, I strongly believe that we were created, not as animals or waste products, but for a divine purpose.

I live by this maxim, and it has changed a lot of things in my nature and brings me to a place of conscious usefulness. This scripture inspires my heart and quickens my inner man each time

I read it. Here it is. Hopefully, it will touch your spirit also. "I will praise thee; for I am fearfully and wonderfully made: marvelous are thy works; and that my soul knoweth right well" (Psalm 139:14). Look at these expressions: FEARFULLY, WONDERFULLY, AND MARVELOUS are attributed to our creative characteristics. That's how the Lord God really sees you. You are his masterpiece; the crowning of his creative genius. After he made you, God had nothing better to create. God rested from his labors. So then, rejoice in your natural birthday, but pitch not your tent on the side of the old nature of evil.

THE MYSTERY OF THE
BIRTH OF THE SPIRIT

Jesus said, "That which is born of the spirit is spirit." You see, as long as we live without the birth of the spirit, according to the Lord Jesus Christ, we are of the flesh—natural, carnal, and sensual. We are without the life of Christ, dead in our trespasses and sins, and cannot really please God even if we want to, because whoever is in the flesh cannot and will not please God.

Our new nature can only be achieved by the birth of the spirit. For better insight, let's see how our Lord Jesus describes this experience. "Marvel not that I said unto thee, ye must be born again. The wind bloweth where it listeth, and thou hearest the sound thereof, but canst not tell whence it cometh, and whither it goeth: So is every one that is born of the spirit." Nicodemus in the natural, though a devout religious leader of his day, could not comprehend this mystery. He thought out loud and said, "How can these things be? Just like him, many are lost, confused, and contentious concerning this experience and saying, how can one be born of the spirit and speak in other tongues?

In the Old Testament we can peak through the window of future events and hear this promise from the Lord God, "Then will I sprinkle clean water upon you, and ye shall be clean: from all your filthiness, and from all your idols, will I cleanse you. A new heart also will I give you, and a new spirit will I put within you: and I will take away the stony heart out of your flesh, and I will give you a heart of flesh. And I will put my spirit within you, and cause you to walk in my statutes, and ye shall keep my judgments, and do them" (Ezekiel 36:25-27). By walking through the corridor of genuine repentance, the Lord promised to put a new spirit within us to empower us, with a righteous desire, to keep his commandments and to do his will. This is not an option or alternative, but the very substance of living a righteous life. It's not of our making, power, or effort, but the divine life of God, engineered by him and now functional in practical living.

This experience ushers in the new nature which now wars against the old nature in our being that had controlled us all these times. The Bible even declares that the angels sing a Happy Birthday song when, even one sinner repents and is born of the spirit into the kingdom of God. Heaven stops and celebrates. Why? Well, it's not easy for a carnal person who had lived all his life for the flesh, to turn to God. When this happens, angels stage a praise and thanksgiving celebration. Hallelujah!!

Also, we read in Joel concerning this mystery of the new birth, when God, through Prophet Joel declares, "And it shall come to pass afterward, that I will pour out my spirit upon all flesh; and your sons and your daughters shall prophesy, your old men shall dream dreams, your young men shall see visions" (Joel 2:28). This is not another spirit of God, but Jehovah God himself pouring out his life into us to live victoriously over and against our old nature. If you have not experienced this, what are you waiting for? The Lord has made this promise to you and will perform it if you believe and desire the birth of the spirit. It's for everyone that believes, regardless of our denominational tag.

It's one of the greatest mysteries in the human relationship with God. "For by one Spirit are we all baptized into one body, whether we be Jews or Gentiles, whether we be bond or free; and have been all made to drink into one Spirit" (I Corinthians 12:13). As a new born child picks up the DNA of the parents by birth, we also inherit the DNA of Christ through this spiritual birth. This is part of the misunderstanding because this birth of the spirit transcends human genealogy. The door is open to all. Through the birth of the spirit we are brought into one body (not two) in Christ Jesus. As the scripture says, "There is one body, and one Spirit, even as ye are called in one hope of your calling; One Lord, one faith, one baptism" (Ephesians 4:4-5).

It's scripturally clear that a Happy Birthday into the family of God is accomplished through a born again experience of the water and of the spirit. Without which **Jesus said you cannot see nor enter into the Kingdom of God.** You can have your name in a religious organization but miss the kingdom of God without this experience. This is your seal to the kingdom, the earnest deposit of your divine inheritance. Make sure you don't miss this. It's written, "In whom ye also trusted, after that ye heard the word of truth, the gospel of your salvation: in whom also after that ye believed, ye were sealed with that holy Spirit of promise, Which is the earnest of our inheritance until the redemption of the purchased possession, unto the praise of his glory" (Ephesians 1:13-14).

"Being born again, not of corruptible seed, but of incorruptible, by the word of God, which liveth and abideth for ever" (I Peter 1:23). We should never short-change God's word for human opinions or philosophies. It's amazing how many have been led astray by humanistic philosophies in the face of the clear word of God. Prophet John the Baptist declared to the multitudes that thronged him, "I indeed baptize you with water unto repentance but he that cometh after me is mightier than I, whose shoes I am not worthy to bear: he shall baptize you with the Holy Ghost, and with fire" (Matthew 3:11). This was a mystery now being revealed to him since no one had experienced it at the moment. It was not a suggestion but a revelation of that which shall take place in the future.

Of course, we know that the natural man, who is of one nature—the old Adamic nature, has problems understanding spiritual insights. That necessitates the birth of the spirit. Only in the spirit can we understand the things that are freely given to us by God. Apostle Paul made a bold declaration when he wrote, "But the natural man receiveth not the things of the Spirit of God: for they are foolishness unto him: neither can he know them, because they are spiritually discerned. But he that is spiritual judgeth all things, yet he himself is judged of no man. For who hath known the mind of the Lord, that he may instruct him? But we have the mind of Christ" (I Corinthians 2:14-16). If you have a problem understanding the new birth teaching, go to the Lord in prayer. Surely, he will give you understanding. He did it for me during my days of ignorance.

WELCOME TO A BRAND NEW LIFE

A true Christian life is not a rehabilitation of the old nature but a transformation—the washing of regeneration and renewing of the Holy Ghost. Happy Birthday in Jesus Christ! You see, your life can never be or remain the same again. The conflicts in the two natures will be profound going forward. We are reminded in the scriptures, "Therefore if any man be in Christ, he is a new creature: old things are passed away; behold all things are become new" (II Corinthians 5:17). You now have a new life, which is Jesus Christ's life in you. No more are you a prisoner to self, flesh, sin, and Satan. The Lord, by his Holy Spirit which you received when he filled you with his person, works mightily in your mortal body to his glory. This is how the Holy Bible says it: "To whom God would make known what is the riches of the glory of this mystery among the Gentiles; which is Christ in you, the hope of glory: Whom we preach, warning every man, and teaching every man in all wisdom; that we may present every man perfect in Christ Jesus: Whereunto I also labour, striving according to his working, which worketh in me mightily" (Colossians 1:27-29). This is our confidence in living a brand new life. Jesus is working mightily in us to bring our fruits unto righteousness. It's not by our might, power, or strength. The old nature is swallowed up by the new as we walk in daily surrender and obedience to the Holy Ghost which we received from God.

Now you can live in victory over the old nature and experience the joy of serving Christ. It's a brand new life. There's no substitute for it. If your experience is biblically sound, all that is said of Christ's life will be evidenced in you. Apostle Paul said, "There is therefore now no condemnation to them which are in Christ Jesus, who walk not after the flesh, but after the Spirit. For the law of the Spirit of life in Christ Jesus hath made me free from the law of sin and death" (Romans 8:1–2). Is that how you feel? Then, praise the Lord for his grace. As a brand new person, you are no more your own; you've been bought with a price—the precious blood of Christ.

Jesus said you shall receive divine power when the Holy Ghost has come upon you; the evidence is speaking in other tongues as the spirit gives you utterance. With this power you are able to tame the old nature when it lifts its ugly head. This is the beauty of it all. We now declare along with Apostle Paul, "I can do all things through Christ which strengtheneth me" (Philippians 4:13). Welcome! Let's fight the good fight of faith and look unto Jesus Christ who has vanquished sin, death, and the grave.

CHAPTER IN A NUTSHELL

- The natural and spiritual births are two unique experiences.
- Every person is born into this world with a sinful nature.
- Human conscience is the gatekeeper to right or wrong, good or bad, and natural or spiritual.
- Our future birthdays are met with joy, sadness, optimism, regrets, etc. depending on the decisions and choices that we make.
- God has endowed upon us an inalienable right to attain usefulness and productive living if we so choose to.
- No matter how sincere we may be, when we're carnally minded, it's impossible to please the Lord.
- The birth of the spirit is not an option or alternative, neither is it a denominational menu item.
- The Holy Ghost is the seal to the Kingdom and an earnest deposit to our divine inheritance.

Chapter Two

Daily Choices

Life's test is given on a daily basis.
You've missed the class if you consider it strange.

There's hardly any day in a person's life that is exactly the same. Each day is predicated upon the choices we make and I realize that there are unforeseen circumstances that could impinge upon our activities. What am I after? Are we totally in control of these choices and decisions? My question to you is profoundly, how do you want this day to end? Whatever your answer may be, are you making the choices, decisions, and engaging in activities that will enable you to achieve your desired end? How do you want today to be different from yesterday? Considering what transpired, do you have any clue?

If you throw your life to chances, you will barely come out with anything constructive. Is there anything that happened yesterday that you wish to improve upon? If there is, waste no moment, get up and tackle it. Now is the best time; moments from now it could be a different story. Bear in mind that two natures are competing for dominance. It's important that you have in place concrete goals that you're working to achieve. I have struggled with so many things in my life but I do better when I sit down to tackle them. Many times the result surprises me. We get better by doing, not by wishing and wondering. Nothing changes just by mere hope that it'll change; there's got to be action applied in the direction of that hope. There and then could we hope for the better.

> *We get better by doing,*
> *not by wishing and wondering.*

Each nature speaks on a regular basis. My observation is that the fleshly nature tends to be louder than the new nature. Is this true with you, also? Oftentimes, seeking to drown everything righteous with the carnal desires seems easy and convenient. This is true, and it's something we face almost on a daily basis. Apostle Paul, in responding to the challenges and carnality of the Corinthian Christians, stressed the fact that, though an Apostle, he dies daily. We must die daily to our fleshly desires to keep from becoming servants again. Again, Apostle Paul said, "For if I build again the things which I destroyed, I make myself a transgressor" (Galatians 2:18). This is a choice we have to make. We cannot rescind this to the Lord. The Lord will give us the grace, but we take the action.

If we are truthful to ourselves, we'll admit that it's a daily battle to live righteously. The two natures are in a vicious, daily conflict. You have to choose to obey one at any particular time. Think about it. If you choose to start the day with Bible reading and prayer, the flesh will immediately come up with another idea. This idea would be totally contrary to what your spirit desired and longed for. It's alarming how many Christians rush from home every morning without spending time in God's presence. Our daily choices and priorities will either make or break us.

CONTENDING DAILY CHOICES

a) Prayer or pleasure

b) Bible reading/study or newspaper, magazines, television, telephone and internet browsing

c) Idleness or productive engagement

d) Witnessing or social compromise with colleagues, family and friends

e) Pursuit of holiness in lifestyle or indulging in carnal desires

f) Catalyst for a godly impact or just trolling along

An important observation to make is that every spiritual choice tends to be a furious fight to carry it out, but the fleshly decisions and choices seem to fly without strings. Sometimes the consequences are subdued by the burning passion of the flesh until the act has been committed. The following verses let us peep into that growing conflict within our being. Pay close attention and meditate upon them. Please do not hurry through these. Ponder on the applications. Here it is, "For we know that the law is spiritual: but I am carnal, sold under sin. For that which I do I allow not: for what I would, that do I not; but what I hate, that do I. If then I do that which I would not, I consent unto the law that it is good. Now then it is no more I that do it, but sin that dwelleth in me. For I know that in me (that is, in my flesh,) dwelleth no good thing: for to will is present with me; but how to perform that which is good I find not. For the good that I would I do not: but the evil which I would not, that I do" (Romans 7:14-19).

These speak a mouthful about this ongoing war in our flesh and spirit. Now, don't forget that this was a man who was mightily used of God to do exploits; a man who built almost half of all early New Testament churches. Upon examination of the tone of Paul's Epistles, we see that the thoughts he expressed in the preceding verses must have kept him humble. I believe that part of his victory over these warring opponents within him was the acknowledgement of the struggle itself. If we don't know the areas of our weaknesses and struggles, how will we better prepare ourselves to confront them?

It's important that you know —

- Your most obvious daily weakness
- How to guard against the dominant thoughts that oppose beneficial spiritual activities
- The daily activities that constantly bring you victory instead of regrets
- The thing that causes you to react carnally before you have time to pray and consider scriptural instructions or ramifications.

- Whom to turn to for counseling, accountability, and support

Your daily choices and decisions are the compass to navigate the complexities of the hurdles that lie in the way to a fulfilled day. You have to be calculative and precise; sticking to your plan of action.

Please note carefully, as I've said on numerous occasions that—

Your hope of tomorrow is mirrored in the activities of today.

How do you conduct yourself when you are away from the church and fellow Christians, in order to avoid becoming a victim of the culture or fleshly lusts? What I have seen is that most of our challenges are centered on the interactions we engage in away from the house of God. Therefore, it behooves us, as Jesus said, to "be wise as serpents and harmless as doves," redeeming the time because each day is spiked with evil.

Do These Things and You Will Be on Top of Your Day

- Be calculative
- Be purposeful
- Be alert and sensitive
- Be watchful and prayerful
- Order your thoughts and actions appropriately

- Walk in the spirit
- Avoid procrastination
- Be thankful

Each day is born new and comes to us with fresh pages to write on. Obviously, it's an opportunity to score new points toward our desired goals. We can neglect it, ignore it, or capitalize upon this brand new day to start afresh. It's a toggle to stay on course because of the battle between the old and the new; between the spirit and the carnal man. Hard as it may seem sometimes, the grace of the Lord Jesus Christ is abundantly able to sustain us through the conflict. We have to be willing to fight the good fight of faith and not succumb to the gnawing cravings of our flesh.

It's a sheer sham to boast of a positive tomorrow when our daily activities are fleshly, carnal, and disgusting. The idea that you will rise up somehow and strike the winning blow is an illusion. Winning is a process, and requires patience, persistence, consistency, and practice to build some ground. What are those challenges in your life from which you emerged victoriously without effort? I'll bet there are not many, if any, to reckon with. What's the point here? **Just this; victory requires commitment and concerted effort on your part.** A day is wasted without a definite plan. Here's what the scripture says, "Boast not thyself of tomorrow; for thou knowest not what a day may bring forth" (Proverbs 27:1).

This is a powerful principle that warrants close attention. Even if you are successful in the early hours of your day, do not sound the trumpet, the day is not over. Do not rush in your mind into tomorrow; there are still some hurdles to tackle for the day. Be patient, unassuming, and alert. Anything can go wrong, that's a fact of life.

TURNING THE PAGE

This means being a conscious, proactive Christian who puts on the whole armor of God daily to do war against the kingdom of darkness. It means realizing that, I'm really a new creature in Jesus Christ and his spirit now works mightily in my being. By faith in his name and exercising spiritual activities, daily victory can be achieved. There's a call for alertness on the basic facts of Christian living. For example, know that the struggle between good and evil; death and life; righteousness and licentiousness go on within us on a daily basis. There's really nothing good in our flesh. This is true regardless of what role you play, the title you have, or the position you occupy in the body of Christ.

Only in our spirit can we obey the law of God. Our flesh, the carnal, sensuous, emotional part of us, cannot please the Lord. How many times have we found ourselves doing something that's out rightly against the clear word of God and in conflict with our new spiritual nature? Do you keep the count? That's why we are to ask the Lord for mercy, not judgment, and plead the blood over our lives regularly.

A truly born again, spirit-filled believer does have the desire, by the spirit of God in them, to please God. Often, our flesh gets us in trouble against our will. This is why we have the altar of mercy to seek for forgiveness and strength. The motions of sin, which war in our old nature can contaminate our spirit if we are careless and unrepentant. There's danger in the lack of Christian accountability. It's a healthy thing to hold oneself accountable to other believers as a safeguard from unruliness and complacency.

It's your daily growth that procures those weeks, months and years of experience. Think of it this way, if you waste your daily time slots and opportunities, does it really matter that many years have gone by? I don't think so; They are just wasted, unproductive years. Apostle Paul admonishes us with these words, "See then that ye walk circumspectly, not as fools, but as wise, redeeming the time, because the days are evil" (Ephesians 5:15-16).

The amplified version of the Bible gives more clarity to this instruction. It reads, "Look carefully then how you walk! Live purposefully and worthily and accurately, not as the unwise and witless, but as wise (sensible, intelligent people), Making the very most of the time [buying up each opportunity], because the days are evil."

STOP AND THINK

- How is your day spent?
- What purpose(s) or goal(s) have you achieved today?
- Would you consider this particular day redeemed (bought back, rescued from being lost) or unproductive?
- Do you often take stock of how your day is spent or don't really pay attention? Please be honest.

18

- In what ways do you think you've made the very most of your daily time allotments?

Since any day could be interrupted, perhaps, each opportunity you capitalize on is equity to your future success. I hold myself seriously accountable as I reflect on my daily time management. When I fall behind, I tend to work harder the next day to catch up, but I can sincerely tell you that it's never easy. The scripture is really true; we must make the most of each day and not waste it. The futility of life demands that we act promptly, wisely, carefully, and diligently if we expect tomorrow to be any better.

Isaiah, the prophet, had a daily routine that guided his day. He says, "With my soul have I desired thee in the night; yea, with my spirit within me will I seek thee early: for when thy judgments are in the earth, the inhabitants of the world will learn righteousness" (Isaiah 26:9). His love for righteousness, in his world, drove him to God's presence early in the day. His early expectation demanded a consistent time with God. He could not wish this into existence without seeking the face of God day and night. He uses the word 'seek' which goes beyond a casual pastime in God's presence.

> *The futility of life demands that we act promptly, wisely, carefully, and diligently if we expect tomorrow to be any better.*

Drawing from my experience and from testimonies of others, I can imagine that Isaiah put up a big fight with his old nature.

19

Consistent, spiritual activity does not sit well with the flesh, not to talk about making it a daily affair. Let me just ask you two simple yet essential questions. (A) How consistent and effective are you with your prayer life? From a score of one to ten where do you think you are? (B) Do you spend up to an hour each day in Bible reading/study? These are some of the vital, Christian daily activities that cannot be shoved away if you plan to be relevant.

These are some of the daily choices we must make that have no substitutes. In order to garner the power and strength necessary to repel the forces of Satan against us, prayer and Bible study must be at the forefront. King David said, "Be merciful unto me, O Lord: for I cry unto thee daily" (Psalm 86:3). He was considered a man after God's heart due to his daily time spent with God and also a tender heart of remorsefulness.

If you want to put the flesh in check and break the clutches of the old nature, prayer and fasting should stand tall on your to-do list. Really, the daily choices you make as a Christian are paramount to living life victoriously in a sin-saturated culture. Remember that we're not angels by any sheer means of the imagination. **We are saved by grace, yes, but we have the flesh, the world, and the devil to contend with.** Apostle Peter proclaimed with a passionate plea, saying to his audience, "Save yourselves from this untoward generation" (Acts 2:40b). Consider the time he wrote this, what would he say about our day, if his day was said to be crooked?

By the grace of our Lord Jesus Christ I challenge us to make right and godly choices in our daily affairs and interactions. Let's not put it off for tomorrow and sit by while the devil and his legions wreck havoc daily against the souls of humanity. May the Lord give us the power to commit to making each day count as we steadfastly wait on him in our watch tower.

CHAPTER IN A NUTSHELL

- Your daily choices and decisions are the compass to navigate the complexities of the hurdles that lie in the way to a fulfilled day.
- It's a sheer sham to boast of a positive tomorrow when our daily activities are fleshly, carnal, and disgusting.
- Since any day could be interrupted by mishaps, each opportunity you capitalize upon is equity to your future success.
- Consistent spiritual activity doesn't sit well with the flesh, not to talk about making it a daily affair, so fight on and have no confidence in your flesh.
- Christian living is a daily affair and there's no other day as important as today.

Chapter Three

Preparation for Battle

*Knowing what to do in time of adversity is the
first step toward victory in life's battles*

S ince we cannot escape ourselves, I believe it's appropriate for
us to be in readiness to subdue every bit of our old nature
by the spirit of Jesus Christ that works mightily within us. By
now you must have discovered that most of your struggles are
not necessarily from third parties but between the old and new
natures within your being. Actually the struggle is a good thing, as
it's a sign that you're truly born again. When I was living in sin my
preparation was how to sin with finesse and without being caught.

Now that Jesus has become the Lord of my life and I've chosen
to live for him until the end of life or when he comes back again,
each day, I prepare to battle my flesh and my carnal desires. A true
soldier who is on the frontline of a battle would not be caught
without his/her weapons of warfare. If that happens, the soldier
is to blame and that's if he/she survives to talk about it. The
application here is no different, as we wrestle not against humans
but against powerful, spiritual, demonic entities that intend to
plunge us into immoral and ungodly lifestyles.

Let's look at this scriptural text together and glean some insights from it. "Forasmuch then as Christ hath suffered for us in the flesh, arm yourselves likewise with the same mind: for he that hath suffered in the flesh hath ceased from sin. That he no longer should live the rest of his time in the flesh to the lusts of men, but to the will of God. For the time past of our life may suffice us to have wrought the will of the Gentiles, when we walked in lasciviousness, lusts, excess of wine, revellings, banquetings, and abominable idolatries" (I Peter 4:1-3). We are called to put on a mind that is prepared to win as Jesus Christ had sacrificed his flesh on Calvary and won the Medal of Honor in victory for us.

We can subdue the lusts of our flesh and bring it under the rulership of the spirit of Christ as the scripture says "But we have the mind of Christ."

(I Corinthians 2:16b). We can no longer commit sin just to satisfy our fleshly lusts, the world, and our human, sensual appetites. The flesh must suffer through fasting, prayer, and willful denial of indulgencies for the spirit to reign supreme. Since Jesus came into our lives, we now have the power, by faith in his finished work, to bring our minds and hearts to execute the will of God. This comes by the process of yielding ourselves to the leadership of the spirit of Christ in us. We don't have to try or struggle to live a Christian life, it's Christ—the anointed one, the resurrected one, that brings the heavenly life to bear in our mortal lives.

When we prepare our hearts and minds in this direction and with this attitude, victory becomes our modes operandi—second nature. Further examination of the above text reveals that at one point in our lives, all we were living for was to indulge in the sinful practices that were in our world—society, culture of influence. That's when Jesus Christ was an outsider or a nominal figure within our realm of religious knowledge. Now, Jesus Christ lives in us to produce the fruit of righteousness by his Holy Spirit. A good comparison would be dropping a sponge in a bowl of water. It simply soaks up the water without resistance because that's the nature of the sponge. Such is the spirit of Christ in us. He absorbs everything spiritual and grieves at everything carnal. That's' why we are instructed not to grieve the Holy Spirit that the Lord has given to us.

You tell me how good and bold do you feel to go into God's presence for prayer when the spirit in you is grieved by a sinful act? Our spirit is always lifted in our lives by righteous living and a conscience void of offense before God and man. We gain back our boldness by honestly confessing and forsaking the act that marred our fellowship.

The battle never ceases, neither should our preparation. As I alluded to earlier, this is an ongoing battle. We should not throw up our arms just because we won yesterday's battles. Today may be more vicious than yesterday. You may need more power than you did yesterday to combat the gnawing, lustful pressure of the old nature. In such regards you cannot afford to overlook the areas of subtle temptations.

IN PREPARATION:

1. We have to maintain a mindset of alertness.

2. Resist, on consistent basis, the notions of sin that war in our members—eyes, mind, ears, emotions, hands, etc.

3. Seek to carry out the will of God in your life by the promptings of the Holy Spirit without delay or resistance. There's no spirit-filled child of God that does not hear the inward witness of the spirit. The problem is obedience and sensitivity.

4. Never forget where God brought you from and the consequences of the life before your salvation. Your change came through genuine repentance from a sinful lifestyle into righteousness.

5. Be mindful that there are witnesses around you. Others will be impacted by your victories or failures.

6. The frontline of this battle is more on the spiritual realm than on the physical.

7. You must mobilize as of necessity and employ all spiritual resources if you expect to come out a winner.

8. Don't play church nor become an EVENT CHRISTIAN. You stand less chance of living a victorious Christian life.

Have no spiritual slackness or laziness in the areas of prayer, fasting, study of the word, fellowship, regular attendance in God's house, and effective witnessing for Christ's sake. Our preparation will help to ward off unexpected attacks by satanic forces whose daily ploy is to take advantage of us. Don't become ignorant of the source(s) of attack. Stop and examine your activities, involvement, association and exposure.

Apostle Peter gave a profound caution as to the debilitating impact of fleshly lusts against the soul. He declares, "Dearly beloved, I beseech you as strangers and pilgrims, abstain from fleshly lusts, which war against the soul" (I Peter 2:11).

Every fleshly lust is at direct war against our soul. There's no room for compromise or oversight. We must abstain from these wars of lusts that wage against our soul. As strangers and pilgrims to the worldly pleasure that have plagued our societies, we must run for cover under the blood of Jesus Christ. Satan uses the lust of the eyes and the lusts of the flesh to bargain for our eternal soul. The Bible says the soul that continues in sin shall die. That's eternal damnation in the lake of fire. Ours is a journey to a fulfilling eternal destiny with the Lord Jesus in glory, therefore, to make it in, we must deny self and all its implicating lusts.

Apostle Paul used an athletic analogy describing his preparation tactics. Here is his statement. "Know ye not that they which run in a race run all, but one receiveth the prize? So run, that ye may obtain. And every man that striveth for the mastery is temperate in all things. Now they do it to obtain a corruptible crown; but we an incorruptible. I therefore so run, not as uncertainly; so fight I, not as one that beateth the air: but I keep under my body, and bring it into subjection: lest that by any means, when I have preached to others, I myself should be a castaway" (I Corinthians 9:24-27).

In essence, if those in the world could muster such discipline to go for the corruptible prize of worldly competition, how much preparation should we avail ourselves with, to make heaven our own? I don't know about you, but I say we must do all that it takes, in spite of our fleshly, carnal tendencies. From his statement here, we see that Apostle Paul's Damascus experience was not enough to keep him from becoming a castaway. If it was so with Apostle Paul, I wonder how we should prepare ourselves to finish this race.

Just like the worldly athletes subject themselves to rigorous training and discipline with a view to winning the race, its incumbent upon us to do more than this to make heaven. Jesus said, "Enter ye in at the strait gate: for wide is the gate, and broad is the way, that leadeth to destruction, and many there be which go in thereat: because strait is the gate, and narrow is the way, which leadeth unto life, and few there be that find it" (Matthew 7:13-14). **We cannot pamper our flesh, celebrate our indulgencies, abuse our liberty in Christ, and be adept compromisers, then boast of being serious, heavenly candidates**.

We must come out, be separate, and touch no unclean thing. It's important we draw the line between good and evil. There's a need to walk the narrow path of righteousness and shun the broad road of pleasure.

LINE IN THE SAND

The children of Israel gave themselves up to all types of abominable practices in spite of God's warning against such. They gloried in their fleshly lifestyles with no regard to the laws of God. It did not go well with them as they were scattered throughout many nations, taken into captivity, and lost the advantage of the Egyptian deliverance. They were instructed by these words, "And that ye may put difference between holy and unholy, and between unclean and clean" (Leviticus 10:10).

> *We cannot pamper our flesh, celebrate our indulgencies, abuse our liberty in Christ, and be adept compromisers, then boast of being serious, heavenly candidates*

They rebelled and followed all manner of the heathen practices that were around them.

Here's Jehovah's exclamation concerning them: "Behold, ye trust in lying words that cannot profit. Will ye steal, murder, and commit adultery, and swear falsely, and burn incense unto Baal, and walk after other gods whom ye know not; and come and stand before me in this house, which is called by my name, and say, We are delivered to do all these abominations?" (Jeremiah 7:8-10). It's amazing how far removed they were from the clear line of demarcation set between them and the heathen nations around. They lost the fear of God and came to his house not with remorsefulness, but with impenitent attitudes. The old nature completely took over their daily lives and it seemed they forgot all the years of bondage, slavery, and cruelty meted out to them in Egypt. God's mercy upon them was abused in many instances, as they went a whoring with the very nations Jehovah God forbade.

Just like them, so much is going on in the churches and places of worship intoday's society, that sometimes one wonders what has befallen us. God's house has been turned into theaters of performances instead of a house of prayer for all people. So much flesh in the church that the world will pale in comparison. The altar has become a playful stage, instead of a place of brokenness and heartfelt search for God's mercy, healing, and forgiveness.

Some people backslide. Pastors and preachers quit the pulpit. Singers and ministers of music commit fornication and adultery. Saved folks fall into immoral, sexual sin. Single folks lust and masturbate. A host of bishops, pastors, and shepherds take their spiritual sons and daughters, in the house of God, defile them, and climb back into the pulpit. Many in Christian leadership are defrauding the churches and their parishioners. It looks ugly right? It's terrible, some may say. It calls for alertness in the body of Christ. The fruit of the flesh is always ugly and shameful.

You may say, 'don't write such things concerning the body of Christ,' but my friends, therein lies the problem. If we are to overcome the flesh, we must be honest and confront the natures that war within us. Besides, it's written, "Examine yourselves, whether ye be in the faith; prove your own selves. Know ye not your own selves, how that Jesus Christ is in you, except ye be reprobates?" (II Corinthians 13:5). The scriptures make it clear that in our flesh—the carnal, sensual, emotional nature, dwells nothing good. Don't make excuses and allowances for your flesh, and ever think that you will escape the bitter consequences.

Truly, we are living in the last days. It's a shame what's allowed today in the altar and in the congregation in the name of Christ. Our flesh is really having a heyday; we need to PREPARE TO MEET OUR GOD. Where do you stand in your life of HOLINESS? Does it really matter to you anymore?

We have so many alternatives for the house of God and everybody is right in their own suggestions, such that God's word does not seem to faze anyone. Moses rejected the pleasures of sin for a season and prepared himself to suffer affliction with the people of God. Folks, we must prepare to die to this world and resist the Laodicean spirit that is permeating our churches. The Scripture says that we should have no confidence in the flesh, if we do, the end result will be costly and painful.

If we prepare to win over our flesh and desires, we will be cautious of our actions. I **cannot be emphatic enough; we live in a sinful world, with sinful people, and we possess a sinful nature**. This nature must constantly be tamed. If not, you'll find yourself back wallowing in the mire. This is not an indictment, but the reality of the battle in our flesh to lord over our spirit. That's why the Bible says that we should always pray and not to faint. The greatest danger of giving the old nature the upper hand is to have no meaningful prayer life. It's a bad place to be, especially when things are not going your way.

During one of the interactive sessions in the course of writing this book, one brother gave his example on how he prepares himself. He said that his problem with fornication was always triggered when he looked at certain parts of a female body. To win this fight, he began to have a new perspective of looking at the sisters as whole persons, not just parts. This approach according to him brought victory over fornicating tendencies. That's why it's important we prepare ourselves ahead of any temptation. There's no need of making a vague boast of a situation you have not yet experienced, thinking you will outsmart the devil and your flesh. Instead, my beloved, have a winning plan in place, because your flesh and mine cannot please the Lord.

A WAKE UP CALL

There comes a time in life that we must do something for any meaningful change to take place. As we wrestle with our old nature to bring fruit unto righteousness and true holiness, we have to forge definite steps to victory.

Apostle Paul made this brazen call, "Finally, my brethren, be strong in the Lord, and in the power of his might. Put on the whole armour of God, that ye may be able to stand against the wiles of the devil" (Ephesians 6:10-11).

Let's hear the Amplified version of the Bible:

> In conclusion, be strong in the Lord [be empowered through your union with Him]; draw your strength from Him [that strength which His boundless might provides]. Put on God's whole armor [the armor of a heavy-armed soldier which God supplies], that you may be able successfully to stand up against [all] the strategies and the deceits of the devil.

> *The greatest danger of giving*
> *the old nature the upper hand*
> *is to have no meaningful prayer life.*

We must be mentally and spiritually prepared to give our flesh, the old nature, and the devil a fight in order for our faith walk to be relevant. We don't want to be as sounding brass, or a tinkling cymbal with no impact, nor without a meaningful testimony that could be a blessing. We have to get beyond blaming the flesh, the human nature, the devil, and others for our lukewarm Christian attitude and lack of godly fear.

Among the Greeks, the parnoplia—full armor, was the complete equipment used by heavily armed infantry. Apostle Paul compared this to the spiritual helps supplied by God for overcoming the temptations of the devil. It's our responsibility to put on all the armor and make no provision for our flesh to fulfill the lust thereof. This shows the seriousness of our need for preparation, to be on the offensive instead of being mowed down by sensuous desires.

We are empowered by the Holy Ghost, which is Jesus Christ in us, working within, to bring all things to the purpose of his will. We draw the strength, through his mighty spirit; to cast down imaginations, bring to silence corrupt and unrighteous thoughts, along with anything that exalts itself against his will in our lives. This is a valiant action, consciously employed on our part to make the devil and all his tactics null and void. If we prepare ourselves, we will have less casualties and regrets in our daily Christian experience. Many have given up in the race and gone back to the world due to repeated setbacks and human failures. Let us be fully reminded that living for Christ requires that we deny ourselves and suit up for battle. Since Jesus Christ declared the victory, we can win over any challenge that comes our way. Put on the whole armor and you shall vanquish in this race in Jesus Name.

CHAPTER IN A NUTSHELL

- Most of our struggles as Christians are not necessarily from third parties but between the old and new natures within us.

- A true soldier, on the frontline of a battle, would not be caught without their weapons, so always arm yourself appropriately.

- We can no longer commit sin just to satisfy our fleshly lusts, the world, and our human sensual appetites and claim to be new creatures in Christ Jesus.

- Don't play church or become an 'EVENT CHRISTIAN.' You stand less chance of living a victorious, Christian life.

Chapter Four

Sources of Temptation and Opposition

Have you ever wondered why, even though you love the Lord with your whole heart, temptations, oppositions, and struggles still sometimes confront you? It could be after a time of passionate prayer, fasting before the Lord, or just coming out of an anointed worship, preaching service. Out of nowhere comes a scathing urge, thought, or pressure of unrighteousness. You are baffled and mutter, 'It cannot be, and I just finished having a great time with the Lord.'

Never forget that, after the Lord Jesus had completed forty days and nights of fasting and prayer, Satan confronted him with fiercely, contested temptations to rob him of the glory of the moment and the benefits of the sacrifice. It was an alarming feat from Satan's vantage point but he lost. Nobody can tempt God and win, but Satan had the audacity to try. From the Lord's teaching, the servants are not greater than their masters, so if the devil tempted God, he will equally tempt us. As we view this very closely, our approach should be no different than our Lord's. We must be armed and prepared to confront satanic temptations steadfastly with faith, rich with the word, and standing on the promises of God.

FALSE EXCUSES

Only when we lack the knowledge of (a) who we are in Christ, (b) the supernatural change that took place after our repentance, (c) the reality of satanic plots against us and (d) the battle between the old and new natures within us, do we make false excuses. The devil sometimes is rewarded undue high marks for being behind almost all our temptations. A closer study of the scripture sheds a different light. Some think they have God to blame, because if he did not allow this, then there's no way I could have fallen into this evil. When that's not enough, it's got to be others who caused them to stumble. If you look closely at the preceding scenarios, you'll notice a pattern. Something or someone is left out. What and who do you think it is, or is the line of reasoning correct as presented above?

As Christians, our ground of authority and affirmations is the holy Bible. I believe it's appropriate to hear what the scripture says as touching this sub-section. Are we together thus far? Even if we're not, it's okay, but let's see what makes us free. We read the following, "Let no man say when he is tempted, I am tempted of God: for God cannot be tempted with evil, neither tempteth he any man: but every man is tempted, when he is drawn away of his own lust, and enticed. Then when lust hath conceived, it bringeth forth sin: and sin, when it is finished, bringeth forth death. Do not err, my beloved brethren" (James 1:13-16).

Let's look closely at what is implied here:

1. There's no justifiable ground for any of us to base such claim.

2. There's no evil-based temptation that comes from God
3. God's nature of holiness exposes evil, so he cannot tempt us at all on this ground.
4. It's the lustful, enslaving desires of our old nature that pulls us to temptation.
5. These lustful, enslaving desires will give birth to sin if we go along, rehearse, and repeatedly fantasize the acts.
6. Then sin with its complicity can result in both physical and spiritual death.
7. It's a great error to make such an excuse.

I see here that what was missing in the process of making excuses was acceptance of personal responsibility and accountability. <u>Our victory over temptations is heightened by alertness</u>. It's obvious therefore, that if we're mindful of the consequences of luring temptations, we'll put up a fight against them.

> ***Knowing what to do in time of adversity is the first step toward victory in life's battles.***

On the other hand, temptation can also reveal how serious and committed we are in our new life of faith. If you appreciate the change that has taken place in your life since your repentance, when Satan tempts you, you'll stand your ground. Instead of looking for excuses, you should do exactly what the scripture says, "Submit yourselves therefore to God. Resist the devil, and he will flee from you" (James

4:7). This is not a suggestion but a statement of fact. When we act upon scriptural commands in faith, the outcome is always phenomenal.

One brother had this to say during one of the sessions. He said that, for months, he battled with lust issues and had to come clean with his wife about this. He said, "the way I dealt with it, was to turn the 'plate down.' I gave myself to prayer and fasting to temper the evil, passionate desires that had bothered and vexed my spirit for awhile."

You know he could have sought for an excuse, kept it a secret from his wife and vaguely promised himself, I'll do no such thing, without taking responsibility and bringing his wife into his struggles. I believe he could have easily fallen a victim to this pressing, lustful desire. **It's not wishes that bring victories in our temptations, but action, concerted, sincere, and proactive actions that are baked in the oven of prayer and fasting.** This process denies the flesh having its way and tending to boss over our desires to please God. Fight the good fight of faith and stop making excuses for your fleshly, carnal and lustful temptations. Know yourself and buckle up for the next round of temptation. There's no escape as long as we live in the flesh in the world of sin.

OTHER SOURCES

Let's look at other sources from the Ephesians narrative. "For we wrestle not against flesh and blood, but against principalities, against powers, against the rulers of the darkness of this world, against spiritual wickedness in high places. Wherefore take unto you the whole armor of God that ye may be able to withstand in the evil day, and having done all, to stand" (Ephesians 6:12-13).

Wow! That's revealing! Do you hear and see what is laid out above? This is not a 'dog fight.' Your opponents are more spiritual than natural. It starts in the spirit realm before the manifestation in the physical realm. If you win in your spirit, it's almost a sure thing that you will come out victoriously in the natural realm.

Principalities—supermudane beings who exercise rule, enforcing their desires in our lives against our will. Evil, fallen angels on a higher hierarchy of leadership in Satan's kingdom. These are prominent players in Satan's kingdom with specific authority and command to execute over other demonic entities. Well-ordered, regimented subjects of evil whose daily responsibilities are to subvert the hearts and minds of humans against the will of God.

Powers—Authorities of the unseen world, yet fully engaged in our affairs both spiritually and physically. Fallen angels under the domain of Satan with enforcing rights to abort God's will and purpose among humans. Their world and activities are as real as ours yet they're covert in operation.

Rulers of Darkness of this World—these are master spirits who wield influence in the darkness of this world. Their antagonistic authority over the affairs of this world is felt through principal leaders of our world. These enjoy the permissive will of God until confronted by spirit-filled believers, who know their authority or till their final judgment day.

Spiritual Wickedness in High Places—spirit forces of wickedness in the heavenlies—supernatural realm. These wicked forces were such that fought against angel Gabriel when he brought answer to Daniel. These can pose as territorial spirits that claim the right over certain area.

Each of the above domain pose a serious threat for any true committed Christian. The incontinency of our nature calls for a daily, prayerful and continuous Christian living. It's my belief that, if the Christian community is property alerted about these forces, we'll be more serious with our journey of faith. Just because I'm a born again, spirit-filled believer, notwithstanding my office in the body of Christ, Satan and his demonic spirits, have not yet been phased out. To be a victorious Christian calls for awareness and diligence of and the sources of attack. We have to contend with these forces on a daily basis, not by our might or strength, but by the Holy Ghost.

In chapter seven of my book, *"When Satan Peeps into Your Future,"* I gave a broad narrative on the *'Landscape of Attacks'*. It's a great chapter to read. Here's the introduction:

> "Our Christian journey calls for diligence and full awareness that we're in an intense spiritual battle. The landscape is massive, contentious and complex, leaving no room for oversight. Much is available to and employed by Satan in this battle as I alluded to in chapter six. Oftentimes, people forget that Satan is a spirit and doesn't operate in a vacuum but through people, forces of nature and even animals in collaboration with demonic host."

I highly recommend you secure this particular title if you're serious about winning this war. Eve lusted for the forbidden fruit and fell; same is true today when lust is allowed to reign in our members unchecked.

One brother had this to say during the discussion for the writing of this book. My wife and I had been discussing the things that could confront us in our walk with God and also those that we've already run into. As I began to be serious about my relationship with Jesus Christ, one day on my job, I abruptly stopped smoking. Some of my friends, whom I smoked with before, started ridiculing me and treating me badly because I no longer went with them. It was rather sad to see their attitude toward me. The way I handled this was to let them know that it was not about them but the problem lies with me, as going with them had become a temptation. I knew where my weakness was. I liked smoking and felt, if I went with them, my old nature could drag me into smoking. My action now is to sit at my desk, read the word, and get soaked in what I'm doing. I was bothered, at first, because they made me feel bad. When I considered that it was the right action to take, I reaffirmed my position, letting them know that I must fight to keep my salvation.

We must face our opposition with courage and not let the pressure force us to compromise our values. This brother's statement reminds me of Apostle Peter's admonition when he said, "Save yourselves from this untoward generation" (Acts 2:40b). You can imagine what he would say today if he was here. This is the issue of knowing our sources of attack and also weaknesses. We are asked, "Can a man take fire in his bosom, and his clothes not be burned? Can one go upon hot coals, and his feet not be burned?" (Proverbs 6:27-28). I hear you say, 'are you kidding?' Of course. NO, that's my position too. We must not dabble in culpable circumstances and expect to come out innocent. It's not a weakness to steer clear of temptations, as much as it's wisdom. In fact, the scripture commands us to abstain ourselves from things that appear to be evil. Notice, it did not say go ahead if you feel or think that you will not become a victim. Instead, don't even give yourself the chance, less you become a victim.

WORLDLY LOVE

The problem of Christians is not God's standard of holiness but the world (system, cultural practices) around us. The children of Israel had the same problem when they entered the promise land. They emerged themselves in the practices of the culture around them against the backdrop of clear warnings from the Lord. "Take heed to thyself, lest thou make a covenant with the inhabitants of the land whither thou goest, lest it be for a snare in the midst of thee. But ye shall destroy their altars, break their images, and cut down their groves" (Exodus 34:12-13). "And the LORD spake unto Moses, saying, speak unto the children of Israel, and say unto them, I am the LORD your God. After the doings of the land of Egypt, wherein ye dwelt, shall ye not do: and after the doings of the land of Canaan, whither I bring you, shall ye not do: neither shall ye walk in their ordinances. Ye shall do my judgments, and keep mine ordinances, to walk therein: I am the LORD your God. Ye shall therefore keep my statutes, and my judgments: which if a man do, he shall live in them: I am the LORD" (Leviticus 18:1-5). It's always easy to please our flesh than to walk in righteousness. How can this be seeing that they suffered for over four hundred years in captivity (Exodus 12:40). We don't have to go too far to discover the answer. Consider yourselves, since the Lord Jesus saved you, the bouts you had to fight with yourselves and the world. It's not a play. It has been real and vicious, right?

Have we not read this scripture before, "Ye adulterers and adulteresses, know ye not that the friendship of the world is enmity with God? Whosoever therefore will be a friend of the world is the enemy of God" (James 4:4). In spite of this clear statement, many of us are unfaithful in our love to Christ. There are many enemies of God in our churches. Just hope you and I are not one. May the Lord help us! How do you know whether you love the world more than Jesus Christ? (a) When you love sports more than church services. Some churches close down their services on Super Bowl night. Others bring in the large screen tv monitors into their family life center to keep the people in church. (b) When you readily spend more on world amusement and demands, yet, neglect the kingdom business, (c) when coming to God's house is a struggle rather than a thing of excitement and thankfulness and (d) when you are silent on the evil perpetuated in our society in order to be accepted.

There are many other aspects of this to mention and I believe you can add to the above. The truth is that our love is to be for Him first, our neighbors second, then ourselves. This is not the case; you know it and I know it, too. I thank the Lord for his mercy and grace, but let's not abuse the liberty. How about this, "Love not the world, neither the things that are in the world. If any man loves the world, the love of the Father is not in him. For all that is in the world, the lust of the flesh, and the lust of the eyes, and the pride of life, is not of the Father, but is of the world. And the world passeth away, and the lust thereof: but he that doeth the will of God abideth for ever" (I John 2:15-17). Wow, all I can say here is, Lord be merciful unto us all.

FOR ALL THAT IS IN THE WORLD . . . ,
❖ **The Lust of the Flesh**
❖ **The Lust of the Eyes**
❖ **The Pride of Life**
. . . Is not of the Father, but from the evil spirits that rule our world

This reminds us that the world is empty, vain and destitute without the true love for God. If we galvanize to the world, its' lust and pride, we will pass away without hope of eternity. We are told that the world, its' lust and pride will pass away with hissing. There's no debate about this. We must therefore fight to keep the faith until the end, humbling ourselves under the mighty power of God. Let's examine ourselves regularly to avert all opposition and temptation and the Lord will sustain us with his right hand of righteousness.

CHAPTER IN A NUTSHELL

- When we sweat through our sacrifice and about to be rewarded, watch out, temptation could be lurking somewhere.

- God's nature of holiness exposes evil, so he cannot tempt us at all with evil.

- It's the lustful, enslaving desires of our old nature that pull us to temptation.

- When we act upon scriptural commands in faith, the outcome is always phenomenal.

Chapter Five

DAMAGING CHAIN OF CONFLICTS

*"For the flesh lusteth against the Spirit,
and the Spirit against the flesh: and these are contrary
the one to the other: so that ye cannot do the
things that ye would" (Galatians 5:17).*

If there's anything we should know by personal experience, by history, by stories, and by witnesses and testimonies of others, it's that no Christian, in spite of their position, is exempt from the battle between the flesh and spirit; between the old and new nature. Granted, as it may be; we all have the responsibility of being in readiness to quench all lustful desires by faith in the name of our Lord Jesus Christ. It's by submitting ourselves under the mighty power of God, through the grace he has provided for us, that we can be sure of winning over these nagging battles.

There's no spiritual utopia in the Christian race whereby you are shielded from the challenges of daily Christian living. Such a mindset would be an opening for satanic advantages. Sometimes, most of us parade ourselves outwardly, as untouchable and invincible, due to successes we have achieved in our ministries or individual lives. This behavior conjures neither an attitude of a peaceful treaty signed with satanic kingdom not to attack us, nor the work of God in our domain. Since this is not possible, why should we ever become presumptuous? The flesh (our natural, carnal, animalistic nature) constantly lusts—evil desires seek to express themselves in our lives through bodily activities. If the Lord has blessed his work in your hands, never allow busy schedules and programs to crowd or replace your personal time in the Lord's presence for prayer, fasting, study, and meditation.

The vicious attacks launched into our minds and hearts (spirits) carry with them a weight of struggles between what we know to do, what not to do, and what we sometimes allow as Christians. The scripture says, "While they promise them liberty, they themselves are the servants of corruption: for of whom a man is overcome, of the same is he brought in bondage" (II Peter 2:19). It's just like Satan promised Eve; that she would be as a goddess, knowing good and evil, with liberty of being self-sufficient. Many today have been deceived by self-serving ministers. Satan, at the time of Eve's temptation, was more subtle than any beast of the field which the Lord God had made as he impersonated the serpent. It was only after Eve yielded to the seduction of the enemy, that she was brought under the bondage of sin and death. Our proper conduct and attitude in this daily battle is to give no place to Satan.

The chain of conflicts may help determine whether we're saved or have mere religion. If we're saved, we'll fight off these attacks to stay saved. If we're not, we'll make excuses, yield to the devil, and quit. The battle line is drawn in the mind, sometimes with higher intensity and urgency. There's no room to be careless or weak in moments such as these, as this will determine success or failure. I have been through these numerous times. What serves me most is the richness of God's word as touching these temptations in my heart. Again, King David said, "Thy word have I hid in mine heart, that I might not sin against thee" (Psalm 119:11).

As we know, there's no substitute for the word of God in the life of a true born-again, spirit-filled Christian. Without the word of God in us, we're mere 'paper weight' Christians in the face of temptations and the enemy of our soul—Satan. It takes time to memorize the word of God but it's a worthy price to pay, considering the alternative and the consequences. Again, the psalmist declares, "Thy testimonies have I taken as an heritage (as my portion) for ever: for they are the rejoicing of my heart" (Psalms 119:111).

The word of God gives us the joy to withstand temptations, for the joy of the Lord is what strengthens us. We need God's word as a soothing balm, especially in times of great challenges, temptations, afflictions, and prevailing obstacles.

UNDERSTANDING THE CHAIN OF CONFLICTS

We should not be surprised as many Christians are, about the chain of conflicts. The Bible says, "For when ye were the servants of sin, ye were free from righteousness" (Romans

6:20). When we lived in sin, righteousness was not expected from us; therefore we didn't have much conflict in our spirit. After repentance and turning our lives to the Lord, the spirit of Christ in us insists on righteousness. This triggers the ongoing conflicts. There are certain things in our lives that we felt should never bother us since we were new creatures in Christ. May be it was so at the beginning, but months and years after, we find ourselves battling with these conflicts again, then we wonder how come. Remember, if you were not saved, should I say, not turned to God, the devil would not bother you. You must understand that since you have surrendered your life to Christ, you are his enemy and he has every right to contend with you.

Have you ever noticed that the more serious you are with living for God, the more temptations Satan brings your way? Sometimes this is frustrating. Please don't be frustrated. As hard as it may seem, know that your promotion time has come. Here's the promise. Lay claim on it; "Blessed is the man that endureth temptation: for when he is tried, he shall receive the crown of life, which the Lord hath promised to them that love him" (James 1:12). Our love for the Lord Jesus Christ sustains us in times of temptations. As we can see in the text just recounted, the blessedness only comes after we have been tried, not before, and we endure the temptation. We must consider and understand that, the light afflictions we face here are not worthy to be compared with the GLORY that shall be. I've heard many Christians actually say that living for the Lord is too hard. They faint, become weary, and give up. Rather, living for self is the most frustrating, vain, and empty life to embark upon. There's

50

hardly a sense of contentment. It's not by our power that we live for him but by his grace. Our flesh cannot serve or please God and we should not depend on it.

Sometimes, it seems that our best efforts don't produce the desired results, and then comes discouragement. Let's read what Apostle Paul said, "For that which I do I allow not: for what I would, that do I not; but what I hate, that do I. But I see another law in my members, warring against the law of my mind, and bringing me into captivity to the law of sin which is in my members" (Romans 7:15, 23). Can you relate to this conflicting tendency? This is Apostle Paul who said that he fasted often. He sold out completely to preach the gospel, yet the old nature of sin was still raging within. He did not quit, but pressed on to finish his course with joy. May the Lord help you and I not to quit in our own time of temptation. There are times in our Christian walk when, against our best intentions, our flesh flatly gets us in trouble. That notwithstanding, we should not give up on our faith. Apostle Paul said that there were times he found himself doing the things that he hated. His attitude was that the old nature was trying to raise its ugly head yet it could not reign anymore. Let's emulate that.

One of the saints related her experience this way. "There's no winning over the flesh without the word of God. Even King David said, thy word have I hid in my heart that I may not sin against thee. Without the word, it's hard to have victory over our flesh. It's not a feeling thing. Many times, I have to rebuke myself due to the thoughts that are warring in my mind. Posing a question to myself, such as, 'are these thoughts glorifying God?'

I've been able to win over a lot of temptations by submitting myself under the mighty power of God, and affirming the word of God in my particular circumstances."

> *There are times in our Christian walk, when, against our best intentions, the flesh flatly gets us in trouble. That notwithstanding, we should not give up on our faith.*

It's obvious that you're not alone in this chain of conflicts, so brave up and be on the offensive. Never bathe in self-pity nor open yourself up to the spirit of discouragement.

Why is it that, after we've been born again, the old man (nature) still wages war within? Responding to this question during a live interactive forum with the saints, one sister gave this input. "The old man is still there to keep me mindful of where I should not be and what I should do. As long as I live, the old man is still there, but when I die the old man will die. Until then, I have to kill the old man daily as Apostle Paul said. In other words, if my flesh tells me to do something, in order to keep it submerged, I do the opposite. That's one of the ways you can confuse the old man; because the voice of the flesh is always louder than the spirit."

What a great statement! The spirit does not savor contention with the flesh. On many occasions, the spirit is quenched if we persist in our fleshly desires. We must know that, as hard as it may seem, we can, by the grace of God and the power of the Holy Spirit, live above the flesh. The world of conflicts intensifies or is subdued based on how we're able to deal with our members—the eyes, ears, hands, mouth, feet, etc. These are the tools that exacerbate sinful activities.

Our flesh will always be subject to our spirit if we exercise the authority we now have in Jesus Christ by his spirit. When we walk in the spirit, the flesh will come along. Never expect your flesh to take the lead of walking in the spirit. You'll be up for a surprise and disappointment. It cannot happen; they're contrary one to another and are at perpetual war with each other.

As I often say . . . ,

When the flesh is enthroned, the spirit is dethroned, and when the spirit is enthroned, the flesh is dethroned.

That's just the way it is. Happy are we and in readiness, if we know these things.

The Israelites backslid against Jehovah and went into abominable idolatries even though they were chosen by God and guided by his presence with continuous signs and wonders. The same is true today. So many who were born again, have slid back into the world and sold their soul willingly to sin and the devil. Apostle Paul once said, "Brethren, be followers together of me, and mark them which walk so as ye have us for an ensample. (For many walk, of whom I have told you often, and now tell you even weeping, that they are the enemies of the cross of Christ: Whose end is destruction, whose God is their belly, and whose glory is in their shame, who mind earthly things.)" (Philippians 3:17-19). It's unfortunate that many people live to gratify fleshly desires and despise the cross of Christ. I pray that the Lord enlighten our spirit to the truth and give us the grace to win over these chains of conflicts.

We must take heed to ourselves and watch carefully these natures within us. Past prayers, fasting, and victories are no grounds of assurance in impeding these warring natures. The Bible says, "Wherefore let him that thinketh he standeth take heed lest he fall" (I Corinthians 10:12). We're to be armed in the spirit of our mind and to be ready to confront every ungodly desire in faith and humility.

CHAPTER IN A NUTSHELL

- No born again Christian, in spite of their position of calling or success, is exempted from the battle between the flesh and the spirit; between the old and new nature.
- There's no spiritual utopia in the Christian race, whereby you're shielded from the challenges of daily Christian living.
- Without the word of God in us, we're mere 'paper weight' Christians in the face of temptations and the enemy of our souls—Satan.
- The more serious you are about living for the Lord, the more temptations Satan tends to hurl on you. Never be frustrated or faint in your mind.

- There are times in our Christian walk when, against our best intentions and efforts, our flesh flatly gets us in trouble. That notwithstanding, we should not give up on our faith. Faith is the victory that overcomes our world of conflicts.

Chapter Six

SATANIC TRAPS

Satan understands and knows of the weaknesses and frailties of flesh and human nature. This knowledge arms him advantageously in setting up traps to either lure us in or catch us off guard in temptations. How many times, as a Christian, have you said "why did I have to do that?" We ask such questions, because we, by the spirit of Christ, know very clearly the difference between right and wrong. This knowledge does not completely hedge us against all the traps of Satan and his demonic host.

These traps could be . . .

- The things we like most to do
- The places we cherish to go; which have no direct religious implication.
- The programs that we may watch. Especially if the spirit of the Lord has placed an alarm within our hearts.
- I've found out that even some phone numbers may become an issue (may open door to lustful conversations).

- Internet surfing and many of the readily available communication gadgets of our modern day.
- The person or group of people that we hang out with on a regular basis.

Satan can find footholds in these areas and cast his bait and set up traps, hoping that we pay no attention, or that we make foolish decisions. We're admonished in the scriptures on this line, "let us lay aside every weight, and the sin which doth so easily beset us, and let us run with patience the race that is set before us" (Hebrews 12:1b). Our cautious attention to what is going on and where we are can restrict us from subtle dangers. <u>It's been my experience that the believer's problem is not really so much of understanding the Hebrew and Greek root meaning of words, as it is knowing how to handle the daily challenges in Christian living</u>.

I hope I'm not misunderstood by those who profess to use the Greek and Hebrew as a bargaining position in their exegesis. Satan does not care how much Greek or Hebrew vocabulary we know, his plot is to derail our commitment to Jesus Christ and cause us to have a shipwreck. If Satan had the audacity to tempt our Lord and Savior, it's certain that he would try to entrap us. Apostle Paul said, "And these things, brethren, I have in a figure transferred to myself and to Apollo's for your sakes; that ye might learn in us not to think of men above that which is written, that no one of you be puffed up for one against another"

(I Corinthians 4:6). I say Amen to that!

Here was a case of outright, horrible immoral lapsity unheard of in those that profess Christ, yet they were engaged in a contention of words to display their wisdom. Satan did not care; he was fine as long as they strove, committed fornication, moved in idolatrous activities, and lived in disunity. Somehow they thought they were still in right standing with God. It's scary, but this happens often among believers. We live in strife with each other while Satan is having a celebration in his kingdom. We better check where we are in Christ, lest we find ourselves wanting like the five foolish virgins without adequate oil in their lamps. What use would it be if, after all, we miss heaven? —God forbid! Apostle Paul admonished, "Examine yourselves, whether ye be in the faith; prove your own selves. Know ye not your own selves, how that Jesus Christ is in you, except ye be reprobates" (II Corinthians 13:5). That's dead serious. Satan goes about on a sinister ambush to trap us; hoping we can stumble and fall into his evil plans. I pray that the Lord give us the spirit of wisdom and revelation in the knowledge of him to counteract all the devices of Satan.

TRADING PLACES

A continuous walk with the Lord will unveil satanic traps around us which may be buried in our daily activities and interactions. II Timothy 2:2 states, "And that they may recover themselves out of the snare of the devil, who are taken captive by him at his will." If we walk in the spirit as the Bible recommends, the snares of Satan will come to light before us. Remembering that our old nature is more sinful than righteous, and plays easily into the traps of Satan, only a diligent walk in the spirit can save us from his ploys.

To Discover and Destroy Satanic Traps Will Demand . . .

1. A daily prayer lifestyle. Fasting on a regular basis to tame the lustful desires of our flesh. Don't deceive yourself. We lust more after terrible areas and things than we will admit.

2. Spending time in the study of and meditation on God's word. This cannot be a once in a while thing if you really want to keep the devil at bay.

3. Being sensitive to the voice of the Holy Spirit in whatever ways he speaks to you. We're all unique and different, so the Lord speaks to us differently and sometimes in similar ways. It takes a careful, close walk with him to identify the way he speaks to you. Once you master it, it's easy to hear and obey, and save yourself lots of painful, inflicting wounds from Satan.

4. Invoking the name of Jesus through the guidance of the Holy Spirit by faith.

5. Applying and pleading the blood of Jesus in absolute faith over the persons, places, or circumstances.

Decisions that we make, which come natural to our flesh, should be watched carefully. It's important to be truthful to ourselves, if we don't want to be ensnared by the devil. If we yield to the Holy Spirit and be sensitive to the divine impressions in our spirit, it becomes easy to tame the carnal passions that wage war in us.

Every spirit-filled Christian does have the witness of the Holy Spirit in their spirit. The Bible declares, "For as many as are led by the Spirit of God, they are the sons of God. For ye have not received the spirit of bondage again to fear; but ye have received the Spirit of adoption, whereby we cry, Abba, Father. The Spirit itself beareth witness with our spirit, that we are the children of God." (Romans 8:14-16). As much as we are born of God by the indwelling spirit, we can now have our fruits unto righteousness. Our flesh therefore does not have to be the medium whereby Satan drags us into captivity. The underlying problem is the willingness to obey the nudging of the Holy Spirit when our flesh is out of control.

Satan only capitalizes upon the grounds we allow, and does a good job at it, too, working at dazzling speed for maximum injury. The important thing to bear in mind is, never give room to the devil. He will trap you into hurtful, costly and painful circumstances. Apostle Paul gave us a clarion mandate when he said, "Stand fast therefore in the liberty wherewith Christ hath made us free, and be not entangled again with the yoke of bondage" (Galatians 5:1). Satan only had a chain upon our neck, when we were the servants of sin, but the yoke has been destroyed because of the anointed power of the Holy Spirit. We are to walk as liberated people in Jesus Christ and avoid all satanic traps. We shouldn't check into his pleasure resort and expect not to bear the brunt of the cost associated therein.

We're also assured that if we stray, the Holy Ghost shall alert us in our folly or error. For it's written, "Let us therefore, as many as be perfect, be thus minded: and if in anything ye be otherwise minded, God shall reveal even this unto you" (Philippians 3:15). Here, we see that, there's no excuse to continue in practicing sinful habits, as the Lord will reveal to us. He will also uncover the traps that Satan has set up for us in sundry ways and places. The dark alley of satanic traps is made clear and open through the light of God's word and the spirit that dwells in us. We cannot continue practicing and indulging in sinful habits, while, at the same time, professing to be new creatures. "What shall we say then? Shall we continue in sin, that grace may abound. God forbid. How shall we, that are dead to sin, live any longer therein?" (Romans 6:1-2). Again we're told, "He that committeth sin is of the devil; for the devil sinneth from the beginning. For this purpose the Son of God was manifested, that he might destroy the works of the devil. Whosoever is born of God doth not commit sin; for his seed remaineth in him: and he cannot sin, because he is born of God"

(I John 3:8-9). God's word is the foundation to our daily Christian living, not our opinions or cultural permissiveness.

> *As much as we're born of God by the indwelling Spirit, we can have our fruit unto righteousness.*

In one of my books, titled, "*When Satan Peeps into Your Future*", I went to great lengths of listing all areas in which Satan can trap us. In chapter six all of Satan's Arsenals are revealed. I highly recommend securing a copy of this book. As I said in chapter six of that book, "My intention is not to overwhelm you but rather to alert you. Hopefully, with patience on your part, after exploring these arsenals, you will take your salvation experience as the best of both worlds and guard it with diligence. It demands your utmost patience, because you may never have stopped to consider Satan's attacks in this light."

> *To avoid being victims of circumstances,*
> *we must be soldiers on the alert.*

There are ongoing, unseen battles in the spiritual realm between the Kingdom of God and of Satan. This battle is more real than we can humanly understand. The scripture teaches us in this light, "For we wrestle not against flesh and blood, but against principalities, against powers, against the rulers of the darkness of this world, against spiritual wickedness in high *places*" (Ephesians 6:12). We must understand the intensity and the dangers of these spiritual forces and be careful not to fall into their sinister traps.

As a case in point, Satan and my flesh know the quality of ladies I appreciate. When he wants to tempt me in this area, of course, he will bring the ladies that possess all these characteristics. He never uses things that you're literally disgusted by to trap you. Satan is wiser than that. All that matters here is that you must know yourself. When the old nature rears its ugly head, if you're not armed, you will trade in your values and compromise in an area that can bring great shame. The new man always seeks to please God, but the old man never desires to please God, and is sensual, earthly and selfish. Don't count on your years of being a born again Christian and let down your guard. Scores of great Christian leaders, who thought otherwise and became complacent, have been brought down to unbelievable consequences. Let's consider our ways, and take heed of what's happening in our lives. Remembering as the scripture says, "A little leaven leaveneth the whole lump" (Galatians 5:9).

Subtle traps of Satan can emerge during difficult times, challenges, and experiences in our lives. Satan always seeks for an occasion, a crack in our relationship, to subvert our faith. The following statement by one of the sisters during the live session leading to this book explains the dangers. She reported it this way, "Myself and my husband have an ongoing problem in our relationship that has not yet been resolved. There's a gentleman on the job that peaks my interest. If the flesh could take over, I would like to know him. When he passes by my desk, I blush and smile as if there's no tomorrow. I had to pray and ask for forgiveness. My spirit would be convicted and I would remember my Pastor's teachings. My protective action has been to get myself engaged in productive activities once I notice him approaching my desk; to keep my attention away from him. I keep myself in prayer to eliminate that lustful, fleshly desire taking over me. My concentration now is on maintaining a healthy prayer life." The honesty of this sister was a great blessing to those in attendance. The fact that she related this experience publicly further strengthens her resolve not to become a victim of satanic manipulations. How honest are you in your often conflicting, fleshly desires?

THE IRONY OF SAMSON'S DOWNFALL

If being chosen by God from the mother's womb could safeguard from satanic traps, then Samson should have never fallen. With divine appointment and responsibility comes commitment and accountability. Samson's mighty conquest as the prophet of God was not enough in diffusing the fiery darts of Satan because he became presumptuous. <u>We do not own the anointed power of God. If we gamble with it, in immorality and stubbornness, the anointing will depart.</u> The Lord's mercy and patience does come to an end. Any person that the Lord chooses to use is on the hit list of Satan. It's sad because sometimes we forget and play into the devil's camp and traps.

Have you found yourself disobeying the Lord against all warnings and cautions? Be honest. What were the consequences and how long did they last?

You possibly regretted all the mistakes, right? But, by then, whatever damage had already taken place. The Israelites were taken captive by the Philistines for forty years because of their unrepentant evil against the Lord their God. During this period God showed mercy to the family of the Danites through Manoah whose wife was barren. The angel of the Lord came with clear instruction to this barren woman: "Now therefore beware, I pray thee, and drink not wine nor strong drink, and eat not any unclean thing: For, lo, thou shalt conceive, and bear a son; and no razor shall come on his head: for the child shall be a Nazarite unto God from the womb: and he shall begin to deliver Israel out of the hand of the Philistines" (Judges 13:4–5).

Destiny was placed upon Samson as the hope of Israel, who will come to deliver them from their enemies. Samson's family found favor in God's sight to be chosen as God's first family. It must have been a great joy to this barren woman, who, previously, must have lost the hope of being a mother. Samson started well to fulfill God's divine appointment. He became so mightily used of God till his presence was a terror to the Philistines.

Wish to God, that we can always continue with the Lord the way we started out. Unfortunately some of us make horrible blunders that lead to ultimate death. I feel for this family, especially this woman, and I feel for Israel also that Samson began to gamble with the anointing. <u>When the Lord begins to work greatly through you, please never forget that Satan hates you, and that the old nature still lusts to envy.</u>

Some people get so stubborn because they feel anointed and disregard wise counsel even of their parents. Sometimes, it's the trap of the enemy, other times, it's our own self-conceited ways. Listen to what the father told him, you would think he should take heed as a man of God. "Then his father and his mother said unto him, is there never a woman among the daughters of thy brethren, or among all my people, that thou goest to take a wife of the uncircumcised Philistines? And Samson said unto his father; Get her for me; for she pleaseth me well" (Judges 14:3). This is the same trap Satan set up for Eve, as we are told that the fruit was pleasing to the eyes. Here, we see that, it was the problem with lust that did him in. Satan's traps have not changed; a lot of Christians are still falling into this old bait, thereby ruining their whole service unto God and humanity.

66

As well-meaning as you may be: "Then when lust hath conceived, it bringeth forth sin: and sin, when it is finished, bringeth forth death" (James 1:15). Samson could not see the destruction that was ahead of him, all he wanted was this eye-catching beautiful woman (it could be a handsome man). As long as God continued to use Samson, he became careless and enticed, even with harlots. You may shrug your shoulders at this, but my beloved brethren, we see this played out day after day in our walk with the Lord.

God's mercy, patience, and longsuffering with us must never be taken for granted. Ultimately, Samson will learn a bitter lesson at the hands of Delilah. Most of you know this story very well. The point I wish to make here is that, this was not an accidental event. With what Samson went through in the hands of this harlot, you would think that, as a man of God, he should have already seen the dangers, repented, and walked away. It's not that easy when you're impregnated with lust and blind to the traps that work beneath the surface. The Bible says: Abstain from all appearance of evil (I Thessalonians 5:22). It does not say go and gamble with evil because you're anointed, and the Lord, by his infinite wisdom, is still using you. I think this is where we make a lot of mistakes and bring hurts and destruction to ourselves and to those that love and respect us. I pray God's mercy and wisdom be multiplied to us in this area.

We do not hurl ourselves in the devil's dungeon and pray for a divine intervention. Just like the flesh, when it's burning with lustful infatuation, it's not dissuaded by special speaking in tongues. Tongues seizes when carnality takes over. The damage is always disastrous. What a horrible end of a mighty man of God, chosen by him from his mother's womb. The devil used Delilah to trap Samson because the old nature was let loose. Very sad, of course, it's never a good picture being the target of the devil's firing squad. Samson's eyes were pulled out because he gave away the secret of his anointing to a harlot. **What a trade-off. Lord have mercy on me! That's what I say, I don't know about you**.

The devil could not be any happier. The one that gave his kingdom defeating blows is housed up in chains and in prison to be used for caricatures to entertain the Lords of the Philistines. I can only imagine what happened to the parents as they watched the inhumane treatment of their prophet, son. Wish to God that Samson was the last victim, but that's far from the truth. Until we learn that, as long as we're in this earthly vessel, we must daily submit ourselves to the lordship of the Holy Ghost, the tears, regrets, and shameful outcomes will not seize. Again the Bible warns us, have not confidence in the flesh. When we lose, the devil gains and the name of Jesus Christ is blasphemed among the unbelievers. I pray God's grace and strength wax mighty in us to thwart all the traps and ambushes of Satan, in Jesus Name.

CHAPTER IN A NUTSHELL

- With divine appointment and responsibility comes caution and accountability.
- We do no town the anointed power of God. If we gamble with it, in immorality and stubbornness, the anointing will depart.
- When the Lord begins to work greatly through you, please never forget that Satan hates you and that the old nature lusts to envy.
- God's mercy, patience, and longsuffering with us must never be taken for granted.
- We do not hurl ourselves in the devil's dungeon and pray for divine intervention.

Chapter Seven

CARNALITY VERSUS RIGHTEOUSNESS

A subverted mind is vain and seeks
to overthrow the knowledge of God
in the conscience and crown it with carnal
humanistic philosophy that bear no substance.

I t's well established in the scriptures and requires no debate that "For to be carnally minded *is* death; but to be spiritually minded *is* life and peace. Because the carnal mind *is* enmity against God: for it is not subject to the law of God, neither indeed can be. So then they that are in the flesh cannot please God" (Romans 8:6-8). What an indictment if we become carnal during our walk with the Lord. Our proper understanding of the meaning of the word itself will shed more light.

According to W. E. Vine Expository Dictionary of New Testament words, we have this definition:

CARNAL: Greek, rendering—
Sarkikos—Sarx—Flesh

Having the nature i.e., sensual, controlled by animal appetites, governed by human nature, instead of by the Spirit of God. Sarkinos in ICorinthians. 3:3
Consisting of the flesh, pertaining to the natural transient life of the body.

So then you can see that, if you live your life on the realm of fleshly, natural desires, controlled by animalist instincts, you cannot please God. It's not possible even when there's a desire to please him, unless you allow the effect of God's spirit to have lordship over your spirit. Carnality thrives when we're consumed with that which satisfies our body (the flesh), the emotions, and the sensuous part of our being. You can never trust the body. As we all know, it's earthly and it's an illusion to expect the corresponding desires to be otherwise.

It's pretty hard to live for our flesh, seeking to gratify our natural transient life of the body and please the Lord at the same time. We're told in Romans 8:7, the carnal mind *is* enmity against God. When we subject ourselves to our carnal mind, we engage in hostile activities against God and his established principles of righteousness. Think about it. At what point in your life do you feel an urge to please the Lord and obey his word? Is it when you're carried over by pleasure or when you're struck with adversity? More often than not, it's when you're facing adversities. The carnal mind, the scriptures say, is not even subject to the law of God nor does it dwell on that realm. I became a born-again, spirit-filled Christian over thirty-eight years ago, yet I'm constantly bringing my carnal nature under the blood and the power of the Holy Spirit. I have paid a high price in so many ways and one thing is sure, carnality and righteousness travel in parallel lines.

You live to learn. I'm still learning. There's no going back to the life of sin and death. Also, I strongly believe that this is one of the determining factors that boost our ability to fight. This fight of faith is one's determination and commitment to eternal life. If it's a recreation for you, you will be a carnally minded person with religious rituals. The Bible says given to a form of godliness, but lack the spiritual impetus to live above the sensual, carnal desires of the old nature.

TEN ATTRIBUTES OF CARNALITY

- Condemnation
- Subject to sin and death
- Weakness in the flesh (feelings and emotions)
- Servitude to fleshly pleasures
- Anti-God attitude
- Natural transient life of emptiness and void.
- Keep the body active—purely sensually.
- Produces heaviness, weight, and feeling of being dirty inside.
- Fleshly bondages and habits.
- Regrets: painful and costly price(s).

Apostle Paul reprimanded the Corinthian brethren for their carnality when he said: "And I, brethren, could not speak unto you as unto spiritual, but as unto carnal, even as unto babes in Christ. For ye are yet carnal: for whereas there is among you envying, and strife, and divisions, are ye not carnal, and walk as men?" (I Corinthians 3:1, 3).

Paul informs us that, as long as we have envying, strife, and divisions, carnality is in operation within us. This is not expected of us who have partaken in the divine nature of Jesus Christ. The operation of these attributes is exacerbated when we fall back into our old nature and suppress the voice of our conscience, which pricks us by the living spirit of Christ in us. It's alarming the number of believers who become so carnal in actions and forget that they have been washed from their old sins. Interestingly, the Lord is very patient and longsuffering. He will restore us back to our right standing and victory over our old nature, the moment we acknowledge our shortcomings and turn to him confessing our sins, and then forsaking them.

It's never the Father's will that we live in carnality as this has a disabling effect on our effectiveness and impact towards those we interact with. To make a life-changing impact over those the Lord brings into our lives, we must put a padlock on the doors of carnality outlets. The Lord would be well served and glorified among the unbelievers as we let the life of Christ be the illuminator and not ourselves. Apostle Paul wrote this powerful inspired statement, "I am crucified with Christ: nevertheless I live; yet not I, but Christ liveth in me: and the life which I now live in the flesh I live by the faith of the Son of God, who loved me, and gave himself for me" (Galatians 2:20).

> *To make a life-changing impact over those the Lord brings into our lives, we must put a padlock on the doors of carnality outlets.*

No wonder this man was greatly used of the Lord to accomplish so much of the New Testament church establishment in which others pale in comparison. Through faith in Christ, we can crucify the old man and allow the Spirit of Christ to live mightily in us. It's absolute necessity that we dread not, neither frustrate the grace of the Lord Jesus in our daily living. His love for us is to see us vanquish over the debilitating pangs of the flesh.

Look at this insight that Apostle Paul instigated here. "For we know that the law is spiritual: but I am carnal, sold under sin" (Romans 7:14). In essence, it takes the spirit to overcome the flesh; the reason being that, the flesh will always incline toward sinful acts. The knowledge of this fact will equip us to yield more to the Holy Ghost within; when there's a dying desire to please the Lord. Each time we do this, we silence the fleshly voices. **There's no winning over the fleshly, carnal desires without (a) knowledge, (b) determined effort, and (c) walking in absolute obedience of the Holy Spirit.**

During one of my presentations, one sister related her experience in curbing the quarrelsome, bitter and divisive spirit that existed in her marriage. This is how she told it to the group: "When I got married, I struggled with the attitude of you did this or that. I had to look out of the box and focus more on myself. Instead of you did this, my approach became, what role did I play in that situation? Majority of the time, the one finger you pointed at others, four had been directed to you. I started focusing more on my role in the situation, which I am doing to better the situation than worsen it. Instead of saying, you and you, I say, my understanding is that something is wrong, and you are upset, let us part ways for now. Our staying here will cause us to say something to each other that we will regret thereafter and create permanent record of hurts in our minds.

Oh what a difference this approach has made in our marriage relationship. The petty quarrels are extinguished, more understanding and peace has returned to our home, thanks to the Lord." This success became possible when she called herself to caution, examined her role and chose appropriate action in resolving the conflicts.

It's true, where sin abounds, grace much more abounds. Sin will lead to carnality but so will the grace of our Lord Jesus in us multiply the seed of righteousness in our lives. Righteousness exalts our lives, so it's safe to say that the walk of faith is the antecedence to righteousness.

Righteousness:

Greek rendering according to W. V. Vine

Dikaiosune'—the character or quality of being right or just. It demonstrates the quality of holiness which must find expression in condemning the acts and practices of sin.

Whatever conforms to reveal the will of God.

We become righteous, not by our self-efforts, but by pledging our faith completely on the finished work of the Lord Jesus Christ. We're complete in Christ, nothing lacking. The work of our righteousness was finished when Jesus shed his blood on Calvary and pronounced, "It is finished." That was it. The quilt of sin that warred in our old nature to bring us to death and condemnation was over. Once we accepted and believed on him by faith, not by our works, we became righteous. We read this word, "For he hath made him to be sin for us, who knew no sin; that we might be made the righteousness of God in him" (II Corinthians 5:21).

Jesus became our substitute lamb that was slain for our sins. This was the wisdom of God in demonstration and it took Satan by surprise. "But Christ being come an high priest of good things to come, by a greater and more perfect tabernacle, not made with hands, that is to say, not of this building; Neither by the blood of goats and calves, but by his own blood he entered in once into the holy place, having obtained eternal redemption for us. For if the blood of bulls and of goats, and the ashes of a heifer sprinkling the unclean, sanctified to the purifying of the flesh: How much more shall the blood of Christ, who through the eternal Spirit offered himself without spot to God, purge your conscience from dead works to serve the living God?" (Hebrews 9:11-14). What a mystery; the unfolding of God's divine plan toward us to reconcile us back to himself. We're washed by his eternal and efficacious blood, constantly sanctified as we plead the blood upon ourselves by faith.

This blood, through the eternal Spirit of God, penetrates our consciences and frees us from dead, carnal desires of the old nature. From within springs forth a passion for righteousness made alive by the spirit of God. It's as we learn to walk in this new nature that carnality is brought under the power of the Holy Spirit. Have you ever noticed that when the anointing power of the Holy Ghost comes upon you, the flesh seizes to bother you at that moment or period? That's the reason the Bible says that if we walk in the spirit, we will not carry out the demands of the flesh.

Let's Examine Attributes of Righteousness:

1. Freedom from condemnation
2. Procures freedom from serving the flesh
3. Secures us right to the spirit of life through Jesus Christ
4. Enables us to walk in the spirit through the eternal operation of the new nature of God in us
5. Produces real joy and peace beyond human comprehension
6. Quickens us through the Holy Ghost to live in the presence of the Lord, though physically here on earth. This is a mystery and overly fulfilling anytime you are in that realm—hallelujah.
7. Empowers our spirit to nullify the demands of the flesh.
8. Provides the key to adoption and joint heirship with Jesus Christ.
9. Provides spiritual witness within our spirit that we are of God.

Carnality will blind us to the benefits and attributes of righteousness, and will also sidetrack us from the path of holiness. Let's not forget for any carnal or fleshly lust that, without holiness, no person shall see the Lord. God is absolutely holy and cannot stand the life of sinful indulgences. To this purpose, he gave us his holy spirit as an enabler. We must be steadfast in our faith and righteous living: "Looking diligently lest any man fail of the grace of God; lest any root of bitterness springing up trouble you, and thereby many be defiled"(Hebrews 12:15).

To free ourselves from carnality and yield to righteousness demands Surrender of our total person—body, soul, and spirit unto him. **Nothing to hold back; give him your all and do not misappropriate his mercy, patience, and longsuffering toward you.** Wake up to righteousness and Christ shall give you light. Don't gamble with your eternal birthright with that which perishes by usage. Carnality and fleshly desires will always carry a costly price and painful consequences and the winning will outlast our earthly life.

CHAPTER IN A NUTSHELL

- If you live your life on the realm of fleshly, natural desires and controlled by animalistic instincts, you cannot and will not please God.
- Carnality will blind us to the benefit and attributes of righteousness, and will also sidetrack us from the path of holiness.

- Righteousness (right stand in Christ) empowers our spirit to suppress the desires of our flesh.

- A profound truth remains in the believers' experience, carnality and righteousness travel in parallel lines. If you serve one, it's not possible to accommodate the other.

Chapter Eight

WINNING OVER
FLESHLY BATTLES

*Don't give in to failure
just because it happened before,
instead learn from it.*

I f you're a true believer, you may have had drawn out battles
with the flesh and possibly lost some. The point is not
whether you have ever lost some battles to your flesh as it is,
learning from that experience. As it is, and as we all know, of
course, I hope so, we can never trust nor have confidence in
our flesh. Our confidence is in the power of the Holy Ghost
that works mightily to strengthen us. Also, in the grace of our
Lord Jesus Christ that becomes our sufficiency. We do have the
power of God within us to win over all fleshly battles. We read
in the scriptures: "According as his divine power hath given;
unto us all things that pertain unto life and godliness, through
the knowledge of him that hath called us to glory and virtue"
(II Peter 1:3).

OUR VICTORY IS PREDICATED UPON:

1. Knowing Jesus Christ as our savior and Lord and knowing the power of his resurrection.
    – As long as Christ has risen from death by the glory of his divine existence, we can live in newness of life, triumphing over our flesh.
2. The divine nature of Jesus Christ that becomes part and parcel of us when we receive the baptism of the Holy Spirit, with evidence of speaking in other tongues.
    – This is the birth of the spirit that Jesus said, it's as a wind that blows.
3. Our completeness in the provision available in and through Christ as we abide in him and him in us.
    – The spirit of life in Christ Jesus, through daily communion with him, frees us from the law of sinful, fleshly practices and death (spiritual and eternal).

Once we're born again of the water and of the Spirit, there are no grounds of excuses to obey and serve our fleshly desires. Here's a powerful truth that we must take to heart: "And ye know that he was manifested to take away our sins and in him is no sin. Whosoever abideth in him sinneth not: whosoever sinneth hath not seen him, neither know him . . . he that committeth sin is of the devil; for the devil sinneth from the beginning. For this purpose the son of God was manifested, that he might destroy the works of the devil. Whosoever is born of God doth not commit sin; for his seed remaineth in him: and he cannot sin, because he is born of God" (1 John 3:5-9). What a great, revealing, and transforming truth. The word of God is that seed in our lives. We cannot practice, nor continue in sin to satisfy our old nature when we are rich with God's word.

> *We don't win over our flesh by trying,*
> *but by believing, yielding, and enriching*
> *ourselves with God's word.*

We're empowered to walk in victory and be the daily light for those in darkness who are engaged in abominable fleshly practices. We're born from above by the power of the Holy Spirit which is the Spirit of holiness that we received from him and cry out Abba-Father. The sign that you're truly born from above and have become a new creation in Jesus Christ is the desire to walk in all pleasing to the leading of the Holy Spirit. You become more passionate and determined to obey the Holy Spirit rather than the fleshly desires.

ACCOUNTABILITY

You will not live a victorious, Christ-like life as a freelance believer. There must be a willingness to be accountable to a church, leadership, a group of committed believers, people in your life that you admire and desire to emulate their walk of faith. This is necessary if you truly desire to win over the gnawing lustful pressures of the flesh.

Remember, no matter how strong you feel as a Christian, two are better than one, the Bible says,

Being accountable is a deterrent to willful submission to sinful practices even as a born again believer. Choose those you respect and are willing to submit to their wise godly counsel. Don't choose your peers if you all are too accommodating to each other.

Let's listen to input by one of my esteemed pastor friends during a live session in the writing of this book: "You have to recognize how important it is to have someone that you are accountable to, whom you have given permission to speak into your life. Someone you really trust, that you can talk to about what you're struggling or dealing with. People who will not criticize you, nor make you feel terrible but support and assist in getting you strong in your faith. Someone who will help build you up to a place of a victorious Christian walk, so, that you don't have to live a defeated Christian life. Though we have the Holy Ghost, we still need somebody, a person in your life, you can share and pray together with; an individual that you will be honest with, accountable to, with complete truthfulness in your Christian walk. The ultimate goal to a true Christian is to make heaven, I don't want to be a church goer, go and shout around the church and miss out with God."

He continued, "While acknowledging the gifts of the Holy Spirit, talk in tongues; I need the people of God to help me be conscious in my faith walk. The Bible says that we should not forsake the assembly. You need the assembly, staying away at home is not appropriate. We need the brethren, how good and pleasant it is for brethren to dwell together in unity. So we need the brotherhood. We need, as I said before, God's people; we need people in our lives that can help us. That's why Jesus told Apostle Peter, 'when thou are converted, strengthen the brethren. In other words, since the Lord has changed your life, then you can be strength, a blessing, and encouragement to others. There are some things that you have overcome, areas in which you are strong and others are not, and vise versa. You can therefore learn the secrets from one another. Such people have won that battle of the flesh in that area and know the way out. There are differences in temptations and how each of us responds to them. What we have to do is learn to sow to our spirit and how to take the spiritual ammunitions and load them up in our spiritual guns, ready to do battle. Load up our guns with spiritual things. The Bible says that if we sow to the spirit, we reap life, but if we sow to the flesh we shall reap death. Our decision is not to sow to the flesh— the natural man. You cannot get that victory in your life if you have been sowing to your flesh. The fact remains that our flesh loves stuff. It loves to be blessed. We're not indebted to the flesh anymore and owe the flesh nothing. We have been bought with a price—the precious blood of Jesus, the Bible says. We're to glorify God in our body and in our spirit." Pastor Ronald W. Sharpe.

These are real truths that the church must emphasize and be honest in their presentation. We're not yet in heaven; therefore the earthly challenges that impede our fruitfulness for the kingdom have to be addressed. That's the only way to win, because we're called to be winners. The Bible says, "Greater is he that is in us, than he that is in the world." The conflicts of the two natures are real. We need to know how to emerge as winners. We have to communicate openly and glean from each other. Learn from others' testimonies and also, use their methods in your life and be a winner. Truth is bitter, but it serves us better to swallow our pride and admit the truth. The knowledge of the Lord Jesus Christ does not automatically free us from the old nature. It's appropriate to ask, can we really live without sin in our old nature? Let's look at the sobering facts.

All types of sinful indulgencies are wide open before us in the body of Christ, more than I can name here. That, not withstanding, if we walk in the spirit as commanded, we shall put to death the desires of the old nature.

THE REALITY

Again, the reality of these conflicts cannot be denied by any true born again believer. Doing so will be a travesty. We read in the Bible, "for the flesh lusteth against the spirit and the spirit against the flesh and these are contrary the one to the other: so that ye cannot do the things ye would." The scripture is very clear about these conflicts. Let's not try to deny them nor paint them. Doing so will jeopardize our chances of winning. Years ago, a Christian brother vehemently refuted the idea of falling into fornication. He did not want to hear such statements as he considered it unimportant. The devil loved that attitude and laid a subtle trap for his assuming righteousness. When he fell into this sin, he was ashamed to talk about it and the devil had him for dinner. It was a bitter, devastating journey for him. The journey to recovery was not easy. He admitted that the cost was overbearing and took years before he could face up to it. He was humbled by this unsuspecting habit which to him was taboo before.

This is the reality. Face up to the truth about the flesh or make a blunder that could be hard to recover. We can always win over the flesh if we're mindful to play by the rules laid down for us in the Holy Scriptures. Consider the departments of the flesh and pay close attention—this is what gives the flesh power to try and rule in some cases and dominate our lives. Let's take a peep: "Now the works of the flesh are manifest, which are these, Adultery, fornication, uncleanness, lasciviousness, idolatry, witchcraft, hatred, variance, emulations, wrath, strife, seditions, heresies, envying, murders, drunkenness, revellings, and such like: of the which I tell you before, as I have also told you in time past, that they which do such things, shall not inherit the kingdom of God" (Galatians 5:19-21). Next time you find yourself serving in any of these departments, remember who your boss is.

The knowledge of the Lord as our Savior does not automatically free us from the yearning of the old nature, so don't be deceived.

FIVE WINNING ACTION PLANS

If you have determined to give the flesh a fight, consider the following:

a) Don't obey the demands of the flesh that contradict God's law.

   • If you choose to neglect this and yield to your emotions, you cannot please the Lord. "So then they that are in the flesh cannot please God" (Romans 8:8).

   • Be careful not to assume that you'll be able to control the outcome when the flesh is charged up. It's always a downward, slippery slope.

b) Walk constantly in the spirit and be prayerful and watchful.

   • Jesus said watch and pray that you enter not into temptation. This calls for a real habit of prayer and circumspection.

   • "This I say then, walk in the spirit and ye shall not fulfill the lust of the flesh" (Galatians 5:16).

c) Don't serve the flesh by carrying out its orders.

   • The flesh can run you wild if you let it, so don't become the errand person.

   • Once again, it's written: "Know ye not, that to whom ye yield yourselves servants to obey, his servants ye are to whom ye obey; whether of sin unto death or of obedience unto righteousness? (Romans 6;16) There it is before us and it matters not what your ministerial title is. If you yield to sin, you are a servant to sin, not to Christ. No person can serve two masters.

d) Die to your flesh and kill its passions.

- If Christ is reigning in our lives by the power of his spirit, we're commanded to: "Mortify therefore your members which are upon the earth; fornication, uncleanness, inordinate affection, evil concupiscence, and covetousness, which is idolatry; for which things' sake the wrath of God cometh on the children of disobedience: In the which ye also walked some time, when ye lived in them. But now ye also put off all these; anger, wrath, malice, blasphemy, filthy communication out of your mouth. Lie not one to another, seeing that ye have put off the old man with his deeds. And have put on the new man, which is renewed in knowledge after the image of him that created him" (Colossians 3:5–10).

- The process can be achieved through fasting, prayer, meditation on God's word, and temperance.

e) Have a hunger to be filled with the spirit on a regular basis. "Blessed are they which do hunger and thirst after righteousness: for they shall be filled."

- It must be more than a want, a thirsting for, having a longing that just does not disappear easily. This allows God's spirit to live the life of righteousness through us with much ease.

A dear sister in response to the discussion of winning over fleshly battles made the following points: "Winning over fleshly battles takes constant fasting and a daily prayer life. It takes knowing the word of God and walking in obedience to the Holy Spirit, even though we don't walk twenty-four seven in the spirit. This notwithstanding, we can invite the spirit of God to strengthen and renew us during our challenges. There have been many occasions on my job that I was tempted to do certain things and really feeling the pressure or the heat. The spirit brought me under strong conviction, saving me from that error and safeguarded outright disobedience within my heart. I felt a deeper warning within saying you cannot do that. I have been saved from many troubles in this way and thank God for the power and leading of the Holy Ghost."

This is our winning mantra, if we utilize it in faith and obedience. The Bible says: "For as many as are led by the spirit of God, they are the sons of God" (Romans 8:14). (and daughters, also). God's spirit is constantly leading his children, but many times we are too absorbed in our issues and activities that we cannot hear. When we mess up, then we return to him and wonder, why was I not listening? That's how it is; we have missed his leading many times and gotten entangled with unnecessary infractions to our hurt and others.

LIVING EXAMPLES AND EXPEREINCES

In order to make this book relevant to the particular circumstances you may find yourselves, I moderated several sessions for input and have included some already. The more we realize that we're not alone in this battle, the better armed we are to fight on to the end. Here are some more excerpts as related by the brethren for you to benefit and learn from the insights.

From Brother Jay C. (not actual name) "To keep my old nature tamed and live victoriously for Christ, the word of God has been my strong defense. If you know the word, it will prick your conscience when you're about to sin. All of us will know, but many times, we carelessly ignore that pricking of the spirit. When you disobey the spirit, be ready for the flocking that will follow. Some of us have these weird ideas, that one service for the whole week can keep us out of temptation and the lustful desires of our flesh."

"It's important that one make themselves present in prayer meetings, Bible Study, and worship services. What I discovered is that, for example, a one month absence from the activities of the church can keep your conscience silent in critical situations. The level of conviction will be subdued because the word of God is not richly implanted in your heart and mind. I hold myself accountable in this area to avoid unwise decisions that will not glorify the Lord. That's why I think we must be steadfast in God's house for refreshing."

Sister Green made these remarks. "When I'm offended, somehow it normally triggers a negative response from me, even though I know it's wrong. To avert that anger, as I sense this strong urging, negative feeling, I develop resistance to the pressure. I will put a check in my mind on it. As the anger rises within me, I will submit myself under the power of the Holy Spirit, so that I do not sin. It has been an area of great challenge for me but God's grace has sustained me in these instances. What I also noticed, is that if

I allow myself to be overcome, sin becomes a natural outcome. I have been able to win over my flesh as long as I submit to the spirit of God."

Jesus Christ died to give us victory over sin, the flesh, and Satan. There is no ground of excuses to remain servants to what we have been set free from. The Lord has assured us in his word that victory is ours if we believe and act upon what we read and hear. "Moreover the law entered that the offense might abound. But where sin abounded, grace did much more abound. That as sin hath reigned unto death, even so might grace reign through righteousness unto eternal life by Jesus Christ our Lord" (Romans 5:20). We, through the unmerited favor of Christ, have increased abundantly by the working of the Holy Spirit to win over the flesh, sin and Satan. As sin seems more commonplace and acceptable in our cultures today, the grace of God is super-abundant and ours for service by faith.

We're overcomers in Jesus Christ. We're called to be victors, not victims, nor slaves to the vices of our flesh, Satan, or sin. We should arm ourselves with that same mind to be exactly what the Bible says we are. Don't settle for any defeat, mistakes, or failures in your life, no matter what the devil suggests. You're a winner. Nothing should have dominion over you as a born again, spirit filled believer. We read, "Ye are of God, little children and have overcome them: because greater is he that is in you, than he that is in the world" (I John 4:4).

We're God's children by faith in Jesus Christ; born again to vanquish in the world that we live and make lasting impacts for Christ. Let's finish the race with patience, pressing toward the marks of the high calling of God in Christ and looking unto Jesus our forerunner.

CHAPTER IN A NUTSHELL

- As long as Jesus Christ has risen from the dead by the glory of his divine existence, you can live in newness of life, triumphing over the flesh, sin, and the devil.

- The Spirit of life in Christ Jesus, through daily communion with him, frees us from the law of sinful, fleshly practices, and death.

- We do not win over our flesh by trying, but by believing, yielding and enriching ourselves with God's word.

- As sin seems more commonplace and acceptable in our world (cultures) today, the grace of God is super-abundant, and ours for service by faith—never forget that.

CONCLUSION

We have come this far by faith and by his grace, isn't that right? We're not going to end up carnally. You're not going to allow the great life in Christ to be evil spoken of; just for a fit of carnality. I know you will not. Your desire is to win here on earth, keep the faith, and be caught up to meet with him in glory or die in faith. "For if in this life only we have hope in Christ, we are of all men most miserable" (I Corinthians 15:19). We're living for and with a purpose. This purpose has eternal values; therefore it supersedes all earthly challenges and attractions.

There's no substitute for a true born again experience. When this is your experience, you lose your pangs for the world and all its vanity. You're in the world but no longer of the world. You've been called out of darkness into the marvelous light of Christ. There's nothing to hide. You're not ashamed to walk into the light, so that your deeds will become the mirror to those who grope in the dark. Thank God the old, dark, and miserable days are past and the new day is dawning. Let's put on the breastplate of righteousness and put to silence the lustfulness of the old nature. "Being born again, not of corruptible seed, but of incorruptible by the word of God, which liveth and abideth for ever. For all flesh is as grass, and all the glory of man as the flower of grass.

The grass withereth, and the flower thereof falleth away: But the word of the Lord endureth for ever. And this is the word which by the gospel is preached, unto you" (Peter1:23-25). Hallelujah! Let's celebrate! The word says we're the righteousness of God in Christ. That's what we are. We can live righteously for God in this present world, not by our power but by the power of God.

Let's shun and reprove the unfruitful works of darkness (flesh) and enjoy the abundant life which Jesus Christ gave us with no apology. Let's make no provision for our flesh to fulfill the lust thereof and Christ shall give us light, and be our light in this dark and sinful world. Never build back the things that you destroyed when you made him your Lord and Savior—including old friends, acquaintances, places, pleasures, music, and idols. It's a clean break; no qualms, no regrets. The change has taken place, forever remain. Hallelujah, you're FREE!

Apostle Paul declared from the top of his lungs and the fullness of his heart: "I am crucified with Christ: nevertheless I live; yet not I but Christ liveth in me: and, the life which I now live in the flesh I live by the faith of the son of God, who loved me, and gave himself for me. I do not frustrate the grace of God: for if righteousness comes by the law, then Christ is dead in vain" (Galatians 2:20-21). Repeat this mantra over and over, love yourself. Let the flesh, sin, and the devil know that you're all for Christ. The son of righteousness shall rise up upon you with healing in his wings. Read this book over, make notes, share it with your friends, and, if you don't mind, let me know how you were blessed.

Fight to the finishing line for Christ has gone before us in victory. Meet you at the altar daily in prayer.

ABOUT THE AUTHOR

Dr. Ephraim John Udofia received Christ as his Lord and Savior on September 23, 1974. He has been in ministry in different roles and responsibilities since 1976. He is a former banker who was in charge of a celebrated Foreign Exchange Department of a commercial bank in liaison with Central Bank.

He was a stock broker with First Investors Corporation holding both State and Federal licenses. Dr. Udofia is the former CEO of Precious Jewels, Inc. which he ran for nineteen years.

Dr. Udofia holds a BSC in Management with a minor in Accounting from Shaw University, Raleigh, North Carolina; MBA from Campbell University, Buies Creek, North Carolina. He earned his Doctorate in Ministry with a major in Missions from the International Bible College and Seminary, Independence, Illinois.

Presently, Dr. Udofia is the Presiding Bishop of Living Faith Apostolic Ministries, an International Mission intensive ministry, both in foreign and home missions. He is an Evangelist by calling with a great passion for the souls of men and women. He has a heart for the mission field. He is, also, an anointed teacher of God's word, financial advisor, motivational speaker and outstanding, dedicated family man. He is happily married with five children.

ORDER FORM

Name _____

Address _____

City _____ State _____

Zip _____

Quantity _____

Total Donation _____

For larger quantities, call 919/961-2589

Make checks and money orders payable to:
Dr. Ephraim J. Udofia

ORDER FORM

For credit card orders, enter your name as it appears on the card:

_____

(Sign name as it appears on credit card)

____¨Mastercard ____ ¨VISA

Card Number_____

Expiration ____/____/_____

Postage/handling: $3.95 per book, call for quantities.

Other Books by the Author:

❖ How To Reap Huge Income in Diamond, Gold and Silver Business—practical hands on business book—$14.95

❖ Ten Commandments of Financial Discipline and Wealth Building—classic wealth series in a nutshell—$3.99

❖ My Mind, Lord—ever struggle to control your thoughts and win the battle of damaging tendencies? The seeds of thoughts you sow will produce its kind. This book is a must for your sanity—$10.99

❖ When Satan Peeps Into Your Future—all satanic schemes will come to light and you will come out a winner. 'Really it makes no difference to Satan whether you won the first, second or third rounds. Be watchful, he'll be back for a licking.'—$11.95

❖ The Mistakes of Debt. Ant Club Financial Seminar—Volume I—If you ever desire beating the debt trap and live debt free, you've to get this book for you library—$14.95

❖ Marriage Landmines You Must Avoid—marriage is an institution with constant renovations and fresh décor. What you put into it will determine your outcome—$11.95

❖ Ants in Action. Ants Club Financial Seminar—Volume II—Discover the ant's mindset and join the investment gurus in their winning secrets—$11.95

❖ Life at Crossroads—many people are fearful of tomorrow which they have not seen, because of where they are today. Fear not!—$2.95

For seminars, crusades, conferences, and/or additional copies, please contact:
Dr Ephraim J. Udofia
Living Faith Apostolic Ministries
Post Office Box 98242
Raleigh, NC 27624
919/872-7518
Visit our web site: *www.missionsonthego.com*
www.life-christian-books.com
www.lfamin.org